CONTENTS

PART I	19
LESSON I: THE UNIVERSE GOES TO WORK	21
LESSON II: THE CALLING	31
LESSON III: SPIRITUALITY GUIDES REALITY	37
LESSON IV: OUR MIND IS LIKE A GARDEN	47
LESSON V: BE HAPPY NO MATTER WHAT	57
PART II	67
LESSON VI: LOVE IS A VERB	69
LESSON VII: FORGIVE	81
LESSON VIII: LOVE YOURSELF	103
LESSON IX: BE THAT MEMORY	117
PART III	129
LESSON X: BE A GREAT HUMAN BEING	131
LESSON XI: DON'T CHEESE PIZZA THIS	139
LESSON XII: BELIEVE	147
LESSON XIII: LET GO AND LET GOD	155
ABOUT THE AUTHOR	181

THE CALLING OF MY SOUL

Life Lessons from the Field Series - Vol. 2

SHEILA TRASK

All rights reserved. No part of this book may be used or reproduced by any means, graphics, electronic, or mechanical, including photocopying, recording, taping or by any information storage retrieval system without the written permission of the author except in the case of brief quotations embodied in critical articles and reviews.

The author of this book does not dispense medical advice or prescribe the use of any technique as a form of treatment for physical, emotional, or medical problems without the advice of a physician, directly or indirectly. The intent of the author is only to offer information of a general nature to help you in your quest for emotional and spiritual wellbeing. In the event you use any of the information in this book for yourself, which is your constitutional right, the author assumes no responsibility for your actions.

Copyright © 2020 Sheila Trask Grand Falls-Windsor, NL Canada All rights reserved.

ISBN 978197774799-0

THE CALLING OF MY SOUL

Dedication

This book intends to bring to life a remarkable woman whom everyone calls Nurse Byrne. People loved to be in her presence, and I think that says it all. The world would be a better place if more people were like her. Nurse Byrne made me want to be a better person. It was because of her I learned to reconnect with my passion and become a happier, more faithful person. I wrote this book with a lot of love and gratitude, to honor Nurse Byrne, and to teach others that greatness comes from within. By reading this book, I hope you learn to live with an open heart and be happy, no matter what life throws your way. Nurse Byrne, I will always be grateful for you and your gift.

8 | THE CALLING OF MY SOUL

"Our memory is a more perfect world than the universe: It gives back life to those who no longer exist."

~Guy de Maupassant

Acknowledgments

Whenever someone writes a book, there are many people involved in the process, and without their help, nothing happens. Initially, to gather information, I put out a request to people I knew to share their comments, thoughts, or stories regarding their lived experience with Nurse Byrne. There were too many responses to mention here, but I would like to thank everyone who spoke with me, left me a message, or referred me to someone else. Your words helped me understand the intensity of the impact Nurse Byrne had on people. There were so many similar comments I decided to use 'student' as the generic author of many quotes to credit everyone without duplication.

Piecing together the life of this beautiful woman meant I had to find people who would help me understand who she was beyond being the school nurse. I did not know her in any other capacity, so I relied on others to fill in the gaps. Nurse Byrne's children, grandchildren, and her nephew graciously shared stories. These stories will touch your heart and help you understand the uniqueness of this woman.

Eugene White shared his enthusiasm for the book with a story about his childhood experience at school. Aiden Mahoney helped me visualize the early life of Nurse Byrne and the town of Harbour Breton, where she grew up. He also took a picture of the benches at Port Harmon and sent me the image to use for my work. He was accommodating and supportive of what I was trying to accomplish. I am grateful for Aiden. He was a beautiful soul who passed before the publishing of this book.

Thanks to Giselle White Borden, who helped me understand the neighbor, Sheila Byrne, and to Monica Gale White for sharing her experience of Nurse Byrne, the Public Health Nurse. Annette Farrell Doody enlightened me on how Nurse Byrne went over and above her call of duty outside of school hours and reminded me there was so much more to Nurse Byrne than I knew.

My biggest regret but much gratitude goes to the late Cathleen Bourgeois, who shared her love and support for this book. When I called her to schedule a time for us to meet, she shared with me that she and Sheila were lifelong friends and had shared many good times and saw each other through many of life's challenges. She seemed to know Sheila Byrne better than anyone and assured me it is a great idea to document the courageous life of this exceptional woman. Unfortunately, that meeting never took place as Cathleen got sick and passed before we could meet. My biggest regret was not recording our first phone conversation, as Cathleen was articulate and forthcoming with her love for Sheila Byrne. She told me they ended their phone calls with one or the other saying, "I love you," and the other responding, "I love you more." Her enthusiasm for this book was encouraging; unfortunately, I was unable to find out more about this great friendship.

I would also like to thank Shirley O'Connor for helping me understand Sheila Byrne in her later years. They became friends through a swim class, so it was intriguing to speak with someone who only knew her as an older woman and a dear friend.

For me, this completed Nurse Byrne's life in Stephenville and the many roles she played. Next, I had to figure out what to do with what I had gathered. Please know if you shared anything with me that gave me perspective or pointed me in the right direction, I am grateful. Even if your story or thoughts are not in this book, I can assure you they helped in a significant way. I hope you take pride in knowing this gift for Nurse Byrne comes from all of us who were fortunate enough to have shared even a small piece of her life.

I am grateful to a few avid readers who did not know Nurse Byrne but were kind enough to give me feedback: Ruth Pfinder, Joanne Drodge, and my sister Phil White for reading my first draft. I was happy to hear that after reading this book, they feel like they know her, and I hope you will too. Special thanks to Glenda McFatridge for her preview encouragement and to Esther Burke for confirming memories. Lastly to Lisa Keough White, a loyal friend and supporter of my work. She read this book aloud with me multiple times during my editing process. Now that is a friend!

Preface

Nurse Byrne was unlike anyone I have ever known. It was in Stephenville on the west coast of the island of Newfoundland, Canada, where I first met her. She was the one 'special person' for many people, who left them in a better place just for having been in her presence.

As a writer, I knew she was 'book worthy.' Nurse Byrne possessed the same characteristics and behavioral patterns of exceptional people, which I had been studying for over 40 years. A living example of how I wanted to live my life, Nurse Byrne lived by the laws of the universe, bringing joy to others, and demonstrating endless strength, faith, and love. It is not enough to know these things or to teach them, you must live them, and she is the person who comes to mind when I think of living your higher purpose. Readers will relate to her on a personal level because her motives were pure, and her story, like her, is real, admirable, and genuine.

I wanted the world to know that an extraordinary woman lived and worked on the island of Newfoundland, in the middle of the North Atlantic, saving lives and saving souls because it was her calling. I hope by telling her story, it inspires others to find their calling and live a life of purpose.

Introduction

Our soul whispers to us, and when we do not listen, it screams at us through events, forcing us to stand up and pay attention. We may have an accident, become fatally ill, or lose a loved one. Our initial response may be anger or intense sadness. We may feel like life is not fair and question why this happened to us. We may become depressed, shutdown, or have thoughts of suicide. However, when we take pain, sorrow, and experience and use it for a higher purpose, our entire life takes on meaning. This new purpose is your calling!

It took me many years of studying to get an understanding of the soul as something other than an unknown entity leaving your body while you transition. I now understand it as an inner voice telling us what we need to know. It reminds us of what we may be ignoring or redirects us toward our purpose in life. Have you ever had an idea pop into your head, and you immediately say to yourself, "Where did that come from?" It is your soul talking!

The idea of writing this book was not some long-contemplated thought or a lifelong dream; it was a soul calling. I was working on two books for my Life Lessons from the Field series when the universe interrupted me. The idea came into my head and out of my mouth on a live Facebook video wishing Nurse Byrne a happy birthday. It was like a sudden burst of energy, an uncontrollable urge to do something. It became my mission and a sense of urgency to write about her.

Nurse Byrne was an 'unconscious healer,' who touched everyone with her loving presence without being aware of the impact she had on people. She was a humble, grateful woman who embraced what life had to offer, whether it was sorrow or joy. By sharing the personal story of her calling, I knew others would benefit, and the mystery of her power would unfold and teach others valuable life lessons. She may have learned these lessons as a child, as a nurse, or perhaps because of her tragic personal life circumstances, but they were golden, and it became my calling to write about them.

This book holds no hidden truths, no juicy tabloid gossip, but it shares stories I created with the help of others based on experiences we had with one of the greatest women who ever lived. It will teach life lessons to you that you may already know but need reminding of so you can become an enlightened person.

The Blessings Are In The Lessons

The Calling of My Soul is a symbolic healing tool that shares stories told through the eyes of those whose lives Nurse Byrne touched. At the end of each chapter, you will find Soul Reflections, a highlight of the life lessons demonstrated through shared experiences. You will also find Soul Whispers, questions your soul needs answering to help you take steps toward your higher purpose. Take this journey with us and awaken your soul to its calling.

PART I

- THE AWAKENING -

LESSON I: THE UNIVERSE GOES TO WORK

"A book, too, can be a star, a living fire to lighten the darkness, leading out into the expanding universe."

~ Madeleine L'Engle

When the universe goes to work, follow it. It starts working the minute we put our thoughts into words, which explains how this book was in the making long before I knew it.

About ten years ago, I was at the Arts and Culture Center in Stephenville when I spotted Nurse Byrne. I had not seen her for a while, so I was excited. We spoke briefly, and then I joined my family.

As I sat there watching her from across the room, I felt this overwhelming love and admiration for her, and I had an uncontrollable urge to tell her how I felt. I followed my hunch and went to the other side of the room, where she stood standing with her friends. I told her how much I admired her, and I thanked her for her kindness to me when I was a child. She smiled as she listened to me going on and on about what a great human being I think she is and how grateful I am for her. As a humble person, she seemed surprised, and her eyes grew bigger as she looked at me in disbelief. She graciously thanked me as if I had just given her a gift. I felt relief, as I had always wanted to tell her how I felt. I hope after reading this book, if there is someone you love or admire, you will feel inspired to do the same.

A couple of years later, my mom passed, and following the funeral, Shirley O'Connor, who had grown up across the street from me came over to me outside the church and said, "There is someone here who wants to see you." I followed her, and to my surprise, it was Nurse Byrne. For a moment, I returned in my mind to the vulnerable little girl standing in line to feel the warmth and love I was about to receive from Nurse Byrne. Broken-hearted over the loss of my mother, I felt as if Nurse Byrne was here to mend me. Being in her presence had a calming effect on me. When she hugged me, I felt safe and comforted, knowing everything would be okay.

I believe that after people cross over, they possess the power to influence life on earth. Through my mother's passing, she arranged a meeting between Nurse Byrne and myself. I regularly wrote after she transitioned, and I felt as if she was influencing my writing. I developed a strong urge to write.

One year later, I had a vision of a book while grading my student's assignments. I saw a book and people smiling as if what they were reading was giving them pleasure and aha moments. I told my students about the vision and that I would write a book and use their work if they wished. The Gratitude Attitude, first published in 2016, is the first book in the series Life Lessons from the Field. All I wanted to do was teach people what I was learning. What I did not realize was the universe was about to teach me a lesson that would change my life forever. My entire life imploded, and I became ill. I found myself barely able to cope. My body was giving out, and my mind was not far behind. I was not able to work; however, writing became my savior and led me back to Nurse Byrne.

Practicing gratitude helped me improve my mental and physical health. Learning to appreciate the quiet and calming my mind allowed me to become fully aware of how out of control my life had become. Gratitude gave me strength, peace of mind, and perspective. It enabled me to change what was not working in my life and taught me to appreciate what I had left when the dust settled.

I developed a three-step process to demonstrate how people can learn the Gratitude Attitude. I remembered telling Nurse Byrne years earlier how thankful I was for her, so I decided to use this experience in the book as an example of how to share gratitude. Unknowingly, I was calling Nurse Byrne back to me. Around the same time that I published the book, I learned that she had been experiencing health challenges. She had moved out of her house in Stephenville to the Silverwood Manor, a senior's home in Kippens, near Stephenville. When I learned of this, I started visiting her.

On my first visit, I gave Nurse Byrne a copy of my book, highlighting where I mention her so she could easily find it. Unbeknownst to me, she had early signs of dementia. She took the book in her hands and admired the cover. She looked at me, and pointing to the author's name on the cover; she said, "I don't know Sheila Trask, do you?" I told her I am Sheila Trask. She looked confused and said, "But I know you." I was confident she knew me because her face lit up with recognition when I entered the room. I knew from personal experience that when a person with dementia no longer recognizes you, they do not respond that way when they see you.

I explained to her that Trask is my married name, and although I am no longer married, I have not changed it back to White. She then nodded and said, "Sure, of course, you are a White. There's a whole crowd of ye." I told her I am like an imposter with many names as my family's name was not

White either as my grandfather's birth name was Alfred Leblanc, not James White, as he was known. She nodded in agreement, as she knew a little bit about the history of the French in Stephenville. We continued our conversation as if the previous one about Sheila Trask had not occurred. She asked about my mother, and I told her she had passed four years earlier. She said, "Yes, sure, that is right. I was at her funeral." I was back to being Sheila White, and the smile on her face said, "I remember you."

Other residents started gathering around, and I could sense Nurse Byrne wanted to keep me for herself, so I asked her if she would like to go outside and sit in the sun. The sun was bright, and I wanted her to be comfortable, so I gave her my sunglasses to wear and told her to keep them, as I knew how much she loved being outdoors. I was trying to return the love she had given me as a child. We had an enjoyable visit, but then I had to go. She always seemed so sad when I would say I am leaving, and that, in turn, made me sad as well. However, the joy she seemed to get when I dropped by made me want to continue to visit her more often, which I did on numerous occasions.

The last time I stopped into the Silverwood Manor, Nurse Byrne was asleep, and a note on her door indicated she was not feeling well. I had brought her some homemade cookies, so I left them and did not disturb her. I was concerned about her health and prayed she would recover. A few weeks later, I contacted her daughter Maureen to see how her mother was doing, and to my surprise, she informed me her mother had moved to Kenny's Pond Retirement Living in St. John's. The move made perfect sense as none of her children lived in Stephenville and St. John's provided easy access by air for her children to come to visit. Her first-born Anne Marie was living just outside of St. John's, so she visited several times a week. The other children lived away but came several times a year to spend one on one time with their mother.

I understood the pain of being away and worrying about your mother. I had gone through that most of my life. Fortunately, my mom was able to remain in her home with the care of my sister Chris, so I could not imagine the worry Nurse Byrne's children were experiencing with their mother living in a retirement home. I later learned they all experienced many emotions; fear, guilt, helplessness, and extreme loneliness for her. Growing up, they had to share her with everyone in the community, so I felt the least I could do was try to give back by visiting their mother.

It was shortly after Nurse Byrne's relocation that I decided to write a book about her. St. John's was four and a half hours away, but I did not mind the drive, and I stayed in a hotel next to where she resided. I soon realized Nurse Byrne's memory was fading fast, so I was not sure if what she was saying to me was real or imagined. I could not separate truth from fantasy because I did not know the difference. I had to figure out quickly what I was going to do about this book, as I had never written a biography, so I had no idea where I was going with the storyline. Fear was my old habit of worrying about pleasing people, and I was not about to let it sabotage this project. Many memories from school were resurfacing for me as I started thinking about growing up in a catholic school system where fear was like a mantra. A few months passed, and while researching for this book, I found a quote by Florence Nightingale, who ironically was a nurse. It said, "How very little can be done under the spirit of fear." With that truth, I decided to park my fear and get to work.

Nurse Byrne was the one who calmed my fears as a child. I felt her reassurance in my heart that I would figure this out, and my instinct was correct. During my next visit with her, I had an epiphany. When I arrived, she was all dressed up and in a great mood. Kathryn, her daughter, had spent the morning with her, and she was still excited about her visit. Nurse Byrne was very talkative, and I loved it. I sat there, listening to her, and I smiled and nodded. All of a sudden, she stopped speaking and said, "I'm sorry I'm talking so much. I guess I'm just happy to have someone to talk to." I assured her I could sit and listen to her talk all day, and that was the truth. I realized although Kathryn had just left, her mother had no memory of it.

Nurse Byrne loved people, and we had a bond that made our conversations flow smoothly. I felt blessed she was talkative that day, as the Nurse Byrne I had remembered spent most of her time listening. She was an exceptional listener, but now I was getting to engage with her on an entirely new level, and she was a great conversationalist. I felt blessed to be in her company, and I found myself wishing I had more times like this with her. It did not matter to me if what she was saying was real or imagined. I enjoyed being with her. I knew after that day how I would approach the book.

I would write stories based on my and others' experiences with Nurse Byrne. I would then take these experiences and creatively turn them into a book that would fit my Life Lessons from the Field series. I did not need facts; what I needed was feelings. I was determined to explore how Nurse Byrne made people feel so that I could get into their character and tell their stories about her. I would share with the world life lessons expressed through stories inspired by Nurse Byrne and the way she approached life. I knew it is not what you do in life, but how you do it, that is important.

This realization was exciting for me, as Nurse Byrne's memory became irrelevant to the book. I was now determined to make the most of every moment I spent with her, and my sensitive side loved the feeling of her energy. Each time I was in her company, I was able to remember and feel the power of her presence, and I was able to incorporate that feeling into my writing.

Knowing how you feel impacts your energy, I could recreate this feeling for readers, and Nurse Byrne's power would continue to eternity. From that moment on, my visits were about enjoying her company and doing whatever I could to make her feel special. I now had clarity and direction, and my focus was to create a book that could change people's lives by passing on Nurse Byrne's mystical healing power.

Several times, I told her I was writing a book about her, and her initial reaction was always the same. She would look concerned, almost afraid, but when I explained to her what the book was about, it seemed as if her fears would go away, and her expression would change. She would then appear humbled. I would tell her how people had such great memories of her and were telling me great things about her. She would ask almost in disbelief, "Did they really say nice things about me?" I would assure her everyone had fond memories of her, and she had a lot to teach the world. Then she would appear to be excited. The smile on her face made this book even more satisfying to write. Not always remembering what people tell you can turn out to be a blessing. We would repeat the above scenario as if it were a rerun. The fantastic joy I felt being able to give her that sense of pride always made the trip to St. John's worthwhile. I felt reassured I was doing the right thing.

Writing **The Calling of My Soul** made me not only learn more about her, but it also allowed me to learn more about my mother, and about myself. Through the eyes of Nurse Byrne, I began to heal from things I did not previously understand. My mom knew how much I loved Nurse Byrne as I had begged her many times to try to remember if she had called me Sheila after her. I was number nine of ten children, so most my mother could remember was that she had heard the name and liked it. Either way, I felt a special connection to Nurse Byrne. As much as I wanted her to hold this book in her hands, I felt something telling me to hold off publishing it. I believe in divine timing, so I knew it would be released when it is supposed to be, and not before. I am so happy that I followed my intuition, as I learned that Nurse Byrne had lots more to teach me long after she crossed over.

Life Lessons From The Field

Soul Reflections: When the universe goes to work, follow it, as you never know where you will end up. When you have a hunch, trust your gut. Our feelings influence our energy, so make sure you surround yourself by people, places, and things that make you feel good. Your feelings are your energy source, so people who make you feel good inadvertently help you reach your highest good.

Soul Whispers

➤ What are you grateful for in your life?

➤ Do you worry about pleasing others?

➤ Do you follow your instincts?

➤ Whom do you know that makes you feel good?

➤ Do you believe in divine timing?

LESSON II: THE CALLING

"There are two great days in a person's life – the day we are born, and the day we discover why."

~ William Barclay

As a child, I learned in the catholic school system that a 'calling' is what someone receives before entering the priesthood or convent.

It separated them from us. It meant they were 'special' to get a 'calling.' I remember being fascinated as I listened to a priest tell my class about his calling. I wondered how God decided who was special enough to get this call and how that calling presented itself.

I awakened early one Sunday morning with the following words repeating in my head, "The Calling of My Soul...The Calling of My Soul." I got out of bed and immediately wrote it down. I have learned from experience that when I awaken with words repeating in my head, they usually mean something. For some reason, I thought this could be the title of this book. I had been unsure what to call it. Something inside of me was telling me to search "The Calling of My Soul," so I decided to google it. I came across a song called 'Fire' by Barns Courtney. The lyrics confirmed I had heard the title of the book at 4:44 on a Sunday morning.

> Sold my soul to the calling Sold my soul to a sweet melody
> Now I'm gone, now I'm gone, now I'm gone Oh gimme that fire
> Oh gimme that fire Oh gimme that fire
> Burn, burn, burn (Courtney, 2020)

As soon as I saw 'burn, burn, burn,' I thought 'Byrne, Byrne, Byrne,' and then I thought about the burning fire that Nurse Byrne had to become a nurse. She may not have sold her soul to the calling, but she certainly did answer the calling of her soul.

I thought back to my recent visit to see her in St. John's. Her daughter Maureen was visiting from Scotland, and we were sitting around chatting, drinking tea, and talking about old times. Maureen took out her iPad and opened the email I had sent her a few months prior. It contained a list of questions I had sent her to help me get information for the book. Maureen decided to ask her mother a few of these questions, and we recorded her answers so that I would have some original quotes.

The first question turned out to be critical to understanding Sheila Byrne, the nurse, but I did not realize it at the time because I had not yet discovered the title of the book. "When did you first know you wanted to be a nurse?" The look on her face said it all. It was almost as if she did not understand the question. Giving it some thought, I realized it did not make sense to her because she had not thought about it. Her response wasn't from a woman with dementia either; it was an honest, lucid response. "I don't know. I suppose I always knew, as I didn't want to be anything else. I only wanted to be a nurse, and the only thing I had to figure out was how I was going to make that happen."

She was very fortunate to have known her 'calling' early in life.

Most of us remember as a child, thinking about what we want to be when we grow up, but hardly any of us become that person. Some people change careers many times throughout their life, while others do not even begin their search. Reflecting on that memory and the repetitive whispers in my ear three months later confirmed the title of this book for me. Nurse Byrne's response and the expression on her face made me realize she had discovered her calling so early in life that trying to recall the exact moment was impossible for her. She was a nurse, that is just who she is, and she did not have to think about it, so the question seemed irrelevant to her.

Your life purpose is not something you find outside of yourself; it is something within you. It is who you are - and that made a lot of sense to me when I applied that thinking to Nurse Byrne.

> *"To be a nurse was the only thing I ever wanted to be. I read a lot, and that might be where I got my ideas. I only ever thought about nursing. I did not know how I would become one, but somehow, I found the way. I never did anything else afterward, and I never wanted to do anything else."*

Your calling is your life purpose. It is not something you decide; it is something you discover, as Nurse Byrne did at a very young age. When you are clear on what you want in life, the clarity of your vision will help you find a way to achieve your life goal. You don't need to know how you are going to accomplish it; all you need to do is decide to go for it.

Nurse Byrne's decision to go for it, was answering the call; and the 'how' unfolded. When you find your purpose, everything falls into place. You begin to live your life with passion, and your work never feels like a job. Perhaps this is why she is acknowledged and remembered as Nurse Byrne by everyone.

"She never worked as a nurse. She was a nurse. It reflected everything she did and how she did it. People still call her Nurse Byrne; that is just who she is," said one neighbour.

I now know a 'calling' is something we all have, but many do not answer it because they allow life to get in their way. Nurse Byrne lived a life of purpose by answering the calling of her soul, and as you will read in this book, she had an inner strength that allowed her to be the best at what she did. She did not let life circumstances detract her from her life purpose, and because of this, many people benefited.

Bringing love into people's lives where none existed, Nurse Byrne demonstrated kindness that left lasting memories. She helped many of us see the good in ourselves, and for that reason, many of us were able to hear our calling. As for my 'small inner voice' saying repetitively, "The Calling of My Soul," it gave me the perfect title for this book.

Life Lessons From The Field

Soul Reflections: Listen to the calling of your soul. It is leading you toward your life purpose. When you answer the call, your journey begins.

Soul Whispers

➤ Do you know your calling?

➤ What do you love to do that seems to make time fly?

➤ What is your inner voice trying to say to you?

➤ What are you passionate about that makes you feel strong emotions?

➤ What is the first step you can take to move toward your higher purpose?

LESSON III: SPIRITUALITY GUIDES REALITY

"Endurance is not just the ability to bear a hard thing, but to turn it into glory."

~ William Barclay

Let your spirituality guide your reality and you will learn to be happy, no matter what happens in your life. One of the reasons I decided to write this book was that I believed Nurse Byrne lived her life in such a way that she intentionally created her results. By staying in control and focussing on what she deemed important in life, she was able to manifest the life she wished for herself and her family. She had learned from a young age that getting what you want in life requires two things: focus and faith. Nurse Byrne seemed to have mastered both, and I was determined to learn this and share it with others.

Despite her sunny disposition, Nurse Byrne's life was far from perfect. She suffered a series of tragedies and had to make some serious decisions. She learned that when adverse things happen, you can choose to fall, or you can choose to rise above and be happy regardless. We learn from our experiences: the good ones and the not so good ones. Nurse Byrne learned we could not control what happens in our life, but we can control how we respond to it.

Sheila Maureen Smith was the second child born to Alphonsus and Mary (Hartigan) Smith on October 10, 1925, in a community known as Harbour Breton on the southwest coast of the island of Newfoundland. Down by the water, there was a series of buildings known as Smith Premises, owned by John Smith and later his son, Alphonsus Smith. They were fish merchants. They bought fish from Fortune, dried the fish themselves, and then exported it to Portugal.

Harbour Breton, considered the capital of Fortune Bay, was home to the Smiths. Fortune Bay, a name one might associate with luck, was not so lucky for the Smiths. In the early 1900s, two of their ships capsized, leaving the Smiths in financial distress. Fortunately for them, they also ran a retail store referred to as Smith's Store, a white building that reached far out over the water. The Smith homestead was a white two-story house next to the store.

Sheila had one older brother, Samuel, who was six years older than her and named after their Uncle Samuel Smith, who was killed in action at Monchy-le-Preux, April 14, 1917, at the age of 27. (First World War Gallery Portraits Index, 2020) She also had two younger siblings, Geraldine, who died at a young age of some unknown illness, and William, also named after one of their father's brothers.

People in Harbour Breton were all the same. No one was any better than another. My father grew up there, and he took over his father's business. He was a smart man, very hard-working, and a great asset to his father's company. We were proud of the family business—even the building was considered 'modern' at that time.

Both of Sheila's parents were blessed financially in comparison to most of the population in the Fortune Bay area, but that did not seem to separate them from the townsfolk. The Smiths, considered friendly people, were known in the community as genuinely kind. Mr. Smith, on many occasions, gave credit to people, knowing repayment was unlikely. People were starving during the 1930s, and he could not turn his back on the townsfolk, so he extended credit to purchase food and other necessary items from the store, which subsequently led to financial hardship for the business and the family. Sheila had a lot of respect for her parents and remembered them fondly. She seemed particularly in awe of her father. She always smiled when she spoke of him.

My father was a special man, an exceptional man. People would knock on our door all hours of the night, pleading for mercy from him, and he never turned anyone away. My mother was quiet, but she was sterner than my father. She hardly said a word, while my father, well, he just loved her. She didn't have to do a thing as he liked to dote on her. I had caring parents who were good people. I had a good life.

Sheila was a very kind, gentle soul like her father. She learned to be empathetic and helpful to other people from him. His generosity kept many people from starvation. I recall Eugene White, a former student from St. Stephen's saying, " If I ever met an angel. I would have to say it was her. I have to be thankful for Nurse Byrne's parents. Whatever made her the way she is, I have to be grateful for it." Later in this book, you will discover why Eugene felt this way.

Sheila described her childhood to me as a happy one.

> *As a child, I loved to play with the local children. We would spend all day swimming in the ocean or playing outside*

> when the weather was good. I loved being out in the fresh air, and that did not change as an adult. I spent as much time as possible outdoors and encouraged my children to do the same.

She swam until she was in her late eighties. Ironically, her physical health forced her to stop. Sheila knew from the time she was a young girl swimming or hanging out on the shoreline that one day she would become a nurse and help children. It was something she found herself constantly thinking about regardless of what she was doing, and seized every opportunity to spend time with children. Nurse Byrne could even recall her first job working with a young child.

> I was only 12 years old looking after a little child. I loved children. I had some excellent jobs after, as I went on to become a nurse so I could work with children. I took any opportunity I could get, so I later went away to Toronto to work. People in Canada had great respect for Newfoundlanders, so getting a job was easy if you left the island because we had a reputation for being good workers. It seemed like people appreciated me everywhere I worked, and because of that, I became a better nurse and a better person.

Aiden Mahoney, also raised in Harbour Breton, admired Sheila Byrne for her determination.

> Sheila was 19 when I was born, so I didn't know her until I moved to Stephenville in the late 1980s, but I was in awe of how she got educated back in a time when it was nearly impossible to get a decent education. I asked her one time how she managed to get through school using nothing but

a slate and chalk. It was a one-room school with only four or five girls. They had one teacher. She told me they got together outside of school and taught themselves. Sheila was bound to be successful as she had the support of her parents. Not many had that back then.

Sheila knew that when you genuinely desire something, it is just waiting for you to acknowledge it and go after it with all your might. Continuing her schooling would require her to move away from home. Her focus was on her fulfilling her dream. At that time, very few children went to school for any period as they had to stay home to help their parents or go away to work.

Getting a high school diploma was very rare. Fortunately, for Sheila, her parents were encouraging and were able to support her in her pursuit of higher education. A saying by an unknown author comes to mind when I think of parenting, "There are two things we should give our children; one is roots, and the other is wings." Sheila got both from her parents and was grateful for the support she received from them.

My father only wanted the best for me. He asked me what I wanted to do and when I told him I wanted to go to Littledale in St. John's to complete high school so I could become a nurse, he said, "very well then." That is all it took. He knew I had a sharp mind, and he supported me in whatever I wanted to do.

Littledale, the former estate of Philip Francis Little, the first premier of Newfoundland, is located on Waterford Bridge Road in St. John's, Newfoundland. In 1883, the Sisters of Mercy purchased it and converted it into a Catholic Boarding school for girls. Sheila moved to St. John's and got her high school diploma from Littledale. She then attended St. Clare's Mercy Hospital School of Nursing. (Archival Moments, 2020)

According to author Catherine Ponder, "Desire is God tapping at the door of your mind, trying to give you greater good." Greater good would come for Sheila. When she graduated, she left St. John's to move to Toronto to work at The Hospital for Sick Children. No one was more suited for this work than Nurse Byrne as she had a great love for children. It was a dream come true for her. Aiden Mahoney recalled her telling him about going away to work.

When she left the island, Newfoundland was not yet a part of Canada. It was before Confederation in 1949, so she had to go through immigration in North Sydney. She had a chest x-ray, and spots showed up on her lungs. The Canadian Border agents tried to deny her entrance into Canada. She worried she would be sent back home with her dreams lost, but she got her way, and they let her through. Later she discovered one of her teachers had been a carrier and infected the students. Many people who grew up during that time, when tuberculosis was common, went through life not knowing they had 'spots' on their lungs but were not contagious; perhaps this was the case for Nurse Byrne.

In 1951 the Hospital for Sick Children moved to its current location on University Avenue. Nurse Byrne helped carry the children to the new site. It was not long after her reputation as an exceptional nurse called her back to Newfoundland. She moved to Corner Brook on the west coast of the island, to head up the Pediatric Unit at Western Memorial Hospital. Corner Brook was to become more than an opportunity to be part of an exciting new hospital unit as it was there she met her future husband, Frank.

At that time, it was uncommon for women to work outside the home once they were married. Sheila wanted to have a family and believed a mother's place is at home with her children. Reluctantly, she gave up her nursing career to find her happily ever after. As much as she loved being a nurse, she did not regret that decision. Sheila would have been content to continue on nursing, but love prevailed. Sometimes the heart wins out over the mind. "When love comes calling, you might as well move out of the way," said Sheila. Smitten by the charming, funny, and good-looking Michael Francis Byrne, she still lit up like a Christmas tree every time she spoke of him. He was born in 1917 in Corner Brook, Newfoundland, to Joseph Byrne and Louise Buckle.

On August 26, 1954, at the age of 29, Sheila Maureen Smith married the love of her life, Frank (as she called him) Byrne. Their best friends, Raymond House and Mercedes Coleman, were witnesses at their wedding, performed by a childhood friend, Reverend G.W. Hull. The newlyweds moved to Stephenville as Frank worked at the Ernest Harmon Air Force Base. They would go on to have five children Anne Marie, Kathryn, Maureen, Michael, and Denise.

Sheila was content to be at home raising her family, but her happily ever after only lasted nine years as in 1963, Sheila's life was about to change forever. She was pregnant with her sixth child when her father, whom she adored, passed away suddenly on April 22. He was 73 years old and had broken his back a few years earlier, so he had lived with a lot of pain. Sheila was heartbroken. Her father had given her unconditional love, and she had leaned on him for everything she wanted in life. She was devastated and deeply saddened by the death of her father and pregnant with a house filled with small children. Life had a few more curveballs to throw her way.

Two months after her father's death, Sheila contracted measles, and her baby was stillborn. She needed a lot of courage to focus on her five children while mourning the loss of her baby. I am sure, at times, it felt too much to bear, but Sheila was a strong woman. Her husband was a loving and supportive partner, so she was able to find comfort in his strength. The love of her family carried her through this terrible nightmare.

When I would visit, our conversations were always positive as she rarely spoke of the sad times in her life. One day out of the blue, she talked about losing a baby as if it were a natural part of life. I, too, had suffered a miscarriage, so I was interested in what she had to say about it. She told me that it was common for women to have miscarriages or stillborn children. I was always conscious of her dementia, so when I visited, I mostly just listened and went wherever she wished to take me. Listening, I became amazed at how willing she was to accept the things she could not change. Sheila said to me, "God must have thought I had enough children to look out to, and knowing what was to come; I guess he was right. He had a plan for me. We can't question those things." I was astonished, those words, frozen in my memory, remind me to have faith and trust that everything is part of a bigger plan. I remember thinking to myself, "Oh Nurse Byrne, you have so much faith and trust in God." I had wondered if it was faith that got her through her misery, and after that day, I found myself compelled to study the power of faith to get a better understanding of its ability to help one cope. This incident sent me on a path of discovery.

Little did she know her life was being redirected back to her 'calling.' It was a tough summer for her emotionally and physically trying to raise five children and deal with her sorrow. Sheila was grateful for her husband's love and support, and as she told me, her five beautiful children kept her going. She was coping as best she could, but the worst was yet to come. Frank, her husband, the love of her life, suffered a heart attack and passed on August 27, just one day after their ninth wedding anniversary. As I write this, I cannot help but think this is the true definition of someone's life blowing up. The pieces fell, and she had to catch them. Once again, confirmation of her life redirected back to the calling of her soul.

Sheila left the hospital that evening and began the long walk home. All the while, she kept thinking to herself, "How am I ever going to tell the children?" Someone picked her up along the way and drove her home. She could not remember who had given her the ride. It is difficult to imagine how a woman would respond to such devastation. She had so much love and faced so much loss in such a short time. The series of accumulated tragedies in such a short period could have sent anyone into a deep depression.

Our plan may not be God's plan. We have to recognize when we need to fight harder and when we need to surrender. Sheila, with her five small children, carried on, despite her losses and her grief. Her husband's family pleaded with her to move to Corner Brook so that she would have the support of family and friends, but she was determined to stay in the home in Stephenville, which she and Frank had made for their family. She cared for their children, and (fortunately for many unknown to her at the time), she decided to go back to nursing to support her family. God has a plan for us, and for Sheila Byrne, it was about to play out.

The universe has a strange way of redirecting us, and sometimes it is challenging to understand, especially in times of grief. A famous quote by author C.S. Lewis sums it up quite nicely, "Hardship often prepares an ordinary person for an extraordinary destiny." Many extraordinary people go through suffering and pain, and it is through their experience that they develop their ability to have compassion and empathy for others. This endurance created some of the most significant healers in the world. Think of Mother Teresa, Mahatma Gandhi, and Nelson Mandela, people who have been through intense pain and suffering but did a lot of good in the world. It takes power not to allow your painful experiences to dominate your thoughts, to focus outside the reality of your pain, and do what you need to do to move forward. I believe we are all teachers at the core of our being, and we cannot teach what we do not know. Perhaps this is why we must endure hard times. Traumatic loss often results in building strength. Sheila Byrne took what she learned from her experience and taught others to be resilient despite what life throws our way.

Life Lessons From The Field

Soul Reflections: Let your spirituality guide your reality as, without it, your life will be a product of what happens to you. Trust everything will work out for your highest good. Take action based on faith, not fear, and watch your life evolve. Get clear about what you wish to obtain in life as clarity brings progress. Be persistent, never give up, and work every day toward your goal. Write affirmations of how you wish your life to be and write them in the present tense as if it is how you are currently living; e.g., I am happy and prosperous.

Soul Whispers

➤ What is your life goal?

➤ Do you have faith, (the absolute belief that things will work out) to help you get started on your journey?

➤ Do you have fears that hold you back?

➤ Are you prepared to continue on your life journey and not let anything stop you?

➤ Do you believe in Divine Timing?

LESSON IV: OUR MIND IS LIKE A GARDEN

"For as he thinketh in his heart, so is he: Eat and drink, saith he to thee: but his heart is not with thee."

Proverbs 23:7

Our mind is like a garden; we reap what we sow. If we plant seeds of positivity in our thinking, we will experience it in our life. But if we plant negativity and anger, we will suffer. James Allen, in his booklet, 'As a Man Thinketh,' claims the body is a servant of the mind, so we need to be the mind by controlling our thoughts; otherwise, they will control us (Allen, 1903).

I continuously study the impact of the mind on the body. I have learned that what we feed our mind feeds our soul, so if we are feeding our soul poorly, it will bring about disease. Knowing this should make us focus our thoughts because they can kill us or make us stronger. After all, our body reacts to our thinking. Look at the damage stress does to the body.

Our mind, consciously or unconsciously, directs our body. Negative thinking over a long period will break your body down just as positive thoughts will build your body up, making you look and feel better. Your thinking, like people, can influence how you think. We must always guard our thoughts, and not associate with negative people, as this will affect our energy.

Focusing your thoughts is also how you accomplish goals. They can be personal goals, such as raising your children to be good people or professional goals, such as obtaining a university degree. The process is the same. In other words, we tell ourselves what to do. Knowing this, we need to be mindful of our thinking. But what happens when life events beyond our control devastate us? Does our life fall apart and we get sick and die? Circumstances can either make us or break us. We have to play the hand we get, so we need to know how to play the game of life. We can't always control what happens to us, but we can control how we are going to respond to it.

Nurse Byrne's third daughter Maureen is a Naturopathic Nutritionist in Edinburgh, Scotland. She is very health-conscious like her mother and is interested in anything related to mental and physical wellbeing. Many people say Maureen is a younger version of her mother. She bears her middle name, and her passion for life is evident in her daily living. Maureen is physically active. She runs every day and loves to teach others the importance of healthy living. She is also curious about how the mind affects the body, given that her family had experienced trauma.

One day I received a message from Maureen, who was concerned about something she had read by Deepak Chopra. He discussed how grief weakens and decreases the function of the body. She was puzzled by the fact that trauma, big or small, can be so devastating to the body but yet her mother, who had suffered much loss, survived, despite, as the book says, it doesn't take much to start destroying your body.

Her mother appeared unaffected, or at least that is what she had put forth to the world. If we behave a certain way long enough, we become that way. In other words, fake it until you make it.

LESSON IV: OUR MIND IS LIKE A GARDEN | 49

You can trick yourself into thinking you are okay, and after a while, you become okay. Many people do not realize that our mind is far more powerful than our bodies. We can accomplish a lot if we choose to ignore our pain and shift our focus to what we desire.

Many would say it was Nurse Byrne's attitude that gave her the ability to move forward and stay focused on her goal of being a good parent and a good nurse. Perhaps she kept herself and her children so busy that she did not have time to grieve, worry, or lose herself in any of the negative energies that would have wiped out most people. She was a survivor in the real sense of the word. She kept her mind and her body active through physical exercise and taught her children to do the same. In many ways, she did what Deepak Chopra teaches people to do to overcome grief. She used a positive approach to life to embrace her pain and to ensure her family not only survived but also flourished.

Maureen sent me an audio message, which I transcribed. I listened to it several times trying to understand what she was saying, and through our emotions, this is what I got,

> *Deepak Chopra says in his book that the tiniest change in energy can lead to massive physical disruption (Chopra, 2009). What does that mean? My mom had a major trauma in her life, but she did not get ill. How did she survive? I know she is an exception to the rule. I have been thinking about it ever since you asked me for an inspirational story. My mom lost her baby in the third trimester of her pregnancy just after losing her father. One month later, on the day after her ninth wedding anniversary, she lost her mate, her life partner. He was the father of her five children. Somehow, she managed to go on. How did she not get sick? How did she survive?*

Nurse Byrne was a courageous woman who fearlessly followed her intuition, 'the still small voice' we read about in the bible. She trusted that her children would be okay because she believed God had a plan for her, and she would follow his lead. Sheila made sure that they never missed an opportunity to celebrate life. She provided a safe, warm place for her children, and guided by faith; she did what she believed God wanted her to do. Maureen continued,

> We came home every day for lunch to a hot meal, even though mom was working. Suppertime, we had another hot meal, and she made everything a special event. We celebrated life as a family. She took the five of us kids for drives all the time. Sometimes it was as simple as going to Corner Brook and checking into the Holiday Inn because it had a pool, so we could all go swimming. That was a special occasion! Many days after work, she took us to the local swimming places like 'Black Bank' and 'Gull Pond.' We would have a perfect picnic. Maybe it was because she loved the water and the outside, and it was her sanity, but she knew how to manage us. She drove us to Prince Edward Island, five kids, and a dog, and we took two ferries to get there. She was a brave woman. Some might call her fearless.

Fear was not on the mind of Nurse Byrne, as her children's wellbeing was her priority. She would not allow her children to suffer deprivation of anything because of their father's death. Determined they would enjoy life, she disciplined them and made sure they became decent human beings. She did whatever it took to make that happen. It did not matter to her what sacrifices she had to make; her children would have the best she could provide and be the best they could be.

> *I fought her lots of times, but she was trying to keep me safe. She did the same for all of us. I admire her. She wanted us to be the very best, speak well, dress well, expand our vocabulary, and be good citizens. She did a fabulous job!*

Expectations are important, as you cannot get what you desire without expecting it. Nurse Byrne was an intelligent and resourceful woman who knew you get what you expect, so she expected nothing but the best. Later in this book, you will see how she used the Law of Expectancy to create for her children, the life she and her husband had desired for them.

Maureen wondered how her Mother had survived without getting ill or falling victim to depression.

> *How did she do it? She was one tough woman! I saw how grief knocked my sister down after losing her daughter. Devastation is the only word I can use to describe it. The pain of losing a child is unbearable, and it made me wonder how Mom, who lost three significant people in such a short period, survived what would have killed most people. So, is she inspirational? Hell Yes! Yes, Mother, You Inspire Me.*

What I notice about Nurse Byrne's children is that each one is special and unique. They all represent a different part of her. None of them is just like her, but just like a particular part of her. If you put them all together, collectively, they are their mother. They all have her glowing smile, but each one shares a special trait. As a family, they represent her strength, her love, and her vitality.

After studying James Allen's work, I became very conscious of paying attention to my thoughts. This perspective made me realize that if we do not like our life, we only need to change our thinking about it, just as Nurse Byrne did for her children (Allen, 1903).

She knew what she had to do, so she began practicing forward-thinking. If she dwelled on the tragedies in her life, it would have had negative consequences for her children. Nurse Byrne, heading in the right direction, knew our thoughts are so powerful they can bring us to our knees or lift us; the choice is ours. She chose to rise and use her positive attitude to create the life she wanted.

Our thinking and approach to life determine the future of those who share our experiences, especially our children. I think Nurse Byrne subscribed to this philosophy. She lived in the present, thereby influencing her children to do the same. Providing a loving and warm environment to feed their minds and their bodies, she instilled the desire to learn and seek new experiences, making life enjoyable for her family. Feeding our minds is equally important to our survival as feeding our bodies. "Our minds are like our stomachs; they are whetted by the change of their food, and variety supplies both with fresh appetite" (Quintilianus, 2020).

Using different theories and laws, many authors agree we influence life by our thoughts and our behaviors. Ralph Waldo Emerson wrote about the Law of Compensation telling us good things happen to good people who face tragedy. In other words, good things happen to reward us for our suffering (Emerson, 2020). There is a similar context in many biblical scriptures that say we will get the grace of God for our pain. If you google what the bible says about the pain people experience, you will find numerous scriptures that discuss how God rewards people who suffer.

Catherine Ponder says the Law of Radiation and Attraction tells us what is to come. "What you radiate outward in your thoughts, feelings, mental pictures, and words, you attract into your life affairs" (Ponder, 2011, p.15). Nurse Byrne's good life may have been compensation for her earlier suffering; however, the way she conducted herself and lived by the laws of the universe influenced the blessings in her life. What she put out into this world came back to her. The stories shared in this book will demonstrate how she invited beauty and good into her life and the life of her children by consciously planning, preparing, and celebrating life.

Through my studies, I have discovered that the Laws of the Universe are the same laws described in the bible. Many authors will not mix scripture or any religious doctrine with personal development. Writing this book, I realized that to understand how people can improve their lives, we must recognize faith, the belief in the unknown. You have to be able to move forward and trust that everything will be okay, or you will never succeed in your goals or survive trauma.

I realized that the only way I could understand Nurse Byrne's actions and mannerisms was to learn to think like her, so I spent endless hours pouring through the pages of my family bible, noting every scripture that brought Nurse Byrne to mind. I learned that biblical scriptures, used in the explanation of universal laws, have the same meaning in their application. Exchange the word 'laws' for the name 'Christ or God or Lord,' and it starts to make sense. 'Universal Laws' are 'God's Laws.' It is fascinating to explore the works of early thinkers and compare their interpretations of biblical applications. "What you sow, you reap" (Galatians 6:7), and the Golden Rule of "Do unto others as you would have them do unto you" (Matthew 7:12). Both are straightforward; some would say common sense, as there are always consequences to our actions, good or bad, but if we live by universal laws, we are more likely to live a good life, which is exactly what the bible tells us.

How you treat others will undoubtedly influence what the universe gives back to you, and Nurse Byrne was a living example.

Her approach to life, despite her grief and sorrow, was one of kindness and love. She was a peaceful person who acted accordingly towards everyone. There is no doubt her thoughts were pure and purposeful, as otherwise, she would not have shown up each day and worked in such a loving, caring manner. Her reward was her children, grandchildren, and the joy of working as a nurse helping thousands of children during her career.

Life Lessons From The Field

Soul Reflections: Our mind is a garden. We reap what we sow. Control your thoughts, and you will control your life. Life is a journey, live it consciously despite what happens. To survive when your world seems like it is falling apart, put one foot in front of the other, and move forward. Things are changing as long as you are doing something, but staying still will eventually lead you backward. Trust that everything will work out for your highest good. Take every opportunity to be good to other people. You must give to receive.

Soul Whispers

➤ Do you focus your thoughts?

➤ What can you do to make every occasion special?

➤ Do you put your best foot forward despite what life throws your way?

➤ Are you a positive person?

➤ What seeds are you planting?

LESSON V: BE HAPPY NO MATTER WHAT

"Therefore take no thought, saying, what shall we eat? Or, What shall we drink?

Or, Wherewithal shall we be clothed?"

~Matthew 6:31

Be happy no matter what life throws at you requires faith. As a grieving widow, and still mourning the loss of her father and her baby, it was often a challenge to put on a brave face for the rest of the world, but more importantly for her children. If Nurse Byrne felt fearful, no one knew it. Her inner strength, guided by her faith, was what people witnessed. Sheila, filled with hope, a natural survivor, was destined for a higher purpose.

The 1960s was a time when most women did not work outside the home, and there were not many supports for single mothers. Sheila not only had to find a job, but she had to figure out how she would get there. She did not have a driver's license and did not know how to drive, but Sheila knew everything would work out as long as she stayed focused on the solution, not the problem. Wavering between hope and fear, she learned to drive, bought a car, drove herself to work, and took her children on excursions. Sheila was not one to feel sorry for herself or to live her life as a victim of circumstances. She was determined to be happy for her children's sake.

> *I did what I had to do to survive, and caring for my children was my priority. I did not have any help raising my family, but I managed with a full-time job. I was determined to be a good parent despite feeling sad my children were going to grow up without their father. I felt sorry for them, as he was a good man. He would come home from work and play with them while I prepared supper. He often bathed them after supper and put them to bed. I loved watching him with the children and hearing them laugh. He loved to make them laugh. I could not help but wonder if any of us could ever laugh again, but for my children's sake, I would do my best.*

Sheila, smiling, in a sad but happy sort of way, often showed emotion in her facial expression as she shared memories with me. Even though it was over 50 years since her husband's passing, it appeared she had remembered it like it was yesterday. It was evident the memories of her husband were not ones she chose to forget. Despite her dementia, she did not forget him or how he made her feel. Later in the book, you will see how she kept his memory alive for their children. There was never a doubt the children's interests were at the forefront of everything she did as a mother. I asked her how she thinks her children would describe her as a parent. She shook her head in wonderment.

I wouldn't want to know. I think I expected a lot of them. I believed expectations are essential. I had the best parents in the world, and when they thought something was 'very good,' that was the way it was. We didn't question that. I only wanted the best for my children. When you are the parent left behind, you hardly have time to think. I did the best I could, and they may not have always understood.

Deciding to go forward and take it one day at a time took strength, but it was how she coped with her new life as a full-time nurse and a widow with five children. Nurse Byrne, persevered, and through the power of her faith, she succeeded. Her focus was on what she needed to do, not on pain of missing her husband as otherwise, she would not have coped.

I was grateful for the way my parents raised me, and I tried to raise my children the same way. I had some fear, worries, and doubt, but I couldn't let that stop me. I had faith everything would work out. I didn't have time to be afraid.

Convinced more than ever of the importance of faith, I was determined to explore this concept. Nurse Byrne, a regular churchgoer, a woman of faith, expressed gratitude for the good in her life and looked for the good in everyone. It was her faith and positive attitude that helped get her through her pain and the days when she might otherwise have given up. By her admission, she had enough faith for the entire family and was able to see the good in her life despite what was happening.

Many people are unable to see past their troubles. They cannot see the blessings they have in their life because of their anger and sadness, especially when they are grieving. Christian author and speaker, Joyce Myer, says, "Faith is a gift from God, whereas doubt is a choice." Happiness comes from within, so it is up to us. The only way we survive is to commit to being happy no matter what happens, and that is precisely what Nurse Byrne did for the rest of her life. Grateful for the blessing of five children, she was determined to figure it all out. She may have had moments of doubt, but her heart, filled with endless faith, knew what was unfolding was all part of a divine plan, so she often thought,

> *Who am I to question this? You see, we do not know our strength until life events test us. Losing my husband required me to rely on faith, to believe everything would be okay, and that is what I did. When it came to my children, I used to think, what if they depend on me and I can't live up to it? It became my lot in life to be that 'special' parent. Many children were allowed to do whatever they liked. I saw the consequences of that kind of upbringing. Sometimes they challenged me, but I had to learn to say no to my children for their best interests. They may not have understood at the time. I did what I thought was best.*

Nurse Byrne knew to say 'no' makes you a far better parent than saying 'yes' and being their friend. No one said parenting is easy, especially when you have to be both mother and father to five and hold up a full-time job. She looked at me as if she had just recalled a time she would never forget. It made me think perhaps there are some things in life you do not forget, regardless of dementia.

Newfoundland women, known for their strength, were the primary caregivers and managed the household while their husbands were working away or, in some cases, passed on. They forged ahead and did what they needed to do. For someone raised in a family considered privileged by many, Nurse Byrne was very resilient. Unlike other young women who grew up during the Depression and forced to leave home at an early age to work in-service to families, Sheila got educated and established a career, a privilege denied to most women of her generation. Despite her lack of experience of the harsh realities of life, Sheila, too, was a survivor. Her strength tested by life events made her grow stronger. She fearlessly made difficult decisions required of a parent. She could not control everything in her life, but she decided how she would react to all the things beyond her control.

Nurse Byrne chose to live life consciously and used the power of choice. She chose to be a great parent to her children, to return to her life as a nurse, and to be a good neighbor. She chose to be happy, no matter what. In every role she took on, she did so with love, kindness, and respect. Determined to be the best in her field, Nurse Byrne became the favorite school nurse.

> *"I remember her being so sweet, and she always had a smile on her face. She must have been a great single parent, as all her children are sweethearts."* Student

In our lifetime, we meet people that help us learn and grow. As a neighbor, remembered for her kindness, she was the favorite parent on the street and served as the neighborhood nurse. When kids got hurt, they ran to Nurse Byrne's house instead of running home. She fixed them up and gave them a treat before sending them along their way. Giving was very comfortable and natural for her, but when someone did something for her, she wanted to show her appreciation by giving back. She did not expect anything for nothing, even from children. Francis Young, a local kid in the neighborhood, shared this memory.

> *I remember myself and Armand White shoveled the h styled driveway at her house back in the early '70s. Two or three feet of snow had fallen. We both earned five bucks*

for our efforts, and that was a lot of money back then. As soon as Nurse Byrne gave us the money, we went to KFC (Kentucky Fried Chicken) for a large box of French fries and gravy, and we still had $3.75 leftover. We thought we were rich. She was kind to us kids on O'Brien's Drive.

Children blessed with her love grew to be grateful and share their stories with others. The safety of Nurse Byrne's home was a warm embrace for many children living in unhappy environments. Kids from several families went to Nurse Byrne's house to escape or perhaps to feel her love or get fresh baked cookies. Children loved her so much that several kids whose mothers had passed or their parents were divorced were secretly praying for their father to marry Nurse Byrne so she could be their mother. I heard that story from one of these children who is now an adult. We laughed when we realized how many others had the same story, and we joked about the tactics the kids probably used in their matchmaking. However, Nurse Byrne was far from interested in finding a husband or a new father for her children. She told her friend, Shirley O'Connor, she only went on one date after her husband passed. Shirley said, "Sheila told me she could not move past the image of her children looking through the window with their sad faces. She decided she did not want to see their little faces like that again, so she never dated or even thought about remarrying."

Our parents are not the only people responsible for us. God sends angels to assist them in looking out for our best interests. Nurse Byrne was one such angel sent to fulfill a need many parents were unable or challenged to meet. Monica Gale White from Stephenville had such an experience. Her story reflects how Nurse Byrne seemed to know what to do and what to say to conquer the fears of a new mother.

◆ ◆ ◆

It Takes A Community To Raise A Child

On Dec 7, 1983, I had a bouncing baby boy. I was in the hospital for three days, and then I went home with this beautiful baby. I was not quite sure what to do with him. I was a new mom, and I did not have a mother or a sister. My mom passed when I was eight years old, and my father raised me. I did not know anything about children or babies, and I didn't even have close friends with children. I felt clueless. I felt incapable and scared that I might do something wrong and damage my baby. I knew I was responsible for him, but I felt helpless and very fearful. A couple of days after getting out of the hospital, I heard a knock at the door, and when I opened it, there stood Nurse Byrne. I cannot tell you how happy and relieved I felt. All I could think was how fortunate for me that my first visit from a public health nurse was the one and only Nurse Byrne. She was like a Guardian Angel sent down to help me. I welcomed her into my home. Although filled with fear, it seemed to pass as she began to show me how to bathe the baby. We talked, and she asked how I was feeling. I am sure she knew I was scared to death. I told her about my fear and how I was feeling, and then something magical happened. Nurse Byrne took my perfectly cleaned baby, wrapped him in a bath towel, and passed him to me. She looked me straight in the eye, and with her beautiful smile, she gently said,

> *Oh, my child, don't you know it takes a community to raise a child? The whole community will help you with this baby. You are not alone. You will never be alone as you have the services of a Public Health Nurse. Aunts, uncles, friends, teachers, and other parents will all be in your child's life. No one raises a child on his or her own. If you have any questions, you know I am always here; ask away.*

◆ ◆ ◆

Making the best of your life, no matter what happens, means you are putting your best foot forward. We become what we wish to be by conscious actions. Nurse Byrne left memorable impressions everywhere she went. We may not be able to measure the power of these impressions, but their long-term impact is undeniable.

Life Lessons From The Field

Soul Reflections: Be happy, no matter what! Have faith, and move forward. While you are busy creating your life, you will leave great memories for those who come behind you. Always expect the best, and you will get the best. Desire and expectancy must become one.

Soul Whispers

➤ Is there someone who could use your help?

➤ How would you like to be remembered?

➤ How can you create lasting memories?

➤ Do you expect the best?

➤ Do you have faith?

PART II

- #LOVE #HEALS -

LESSON VI: LOVE IS A VERB

"There is for each [woman], perfect self-expression. There is a place which [she] is to fill, and no one else can fill, something which [she] is to do, which no one else can do; it is [her] destiny!"

~ Florence Scovel Shinn

Work was scarce after the Ernest Harmon Air Force Base closed in 1966. The exciting nightlife that the locals and Americans enjoyed for several decades was now a mere memory. After the Americans left, so did a lot of families, businesses, and jobs. The town of Stephenville suffered so much loss it became a ghost town. For many of the families that stayed, poverty set in, shaking families to the core. Families with limited resources focussed on survival, not embracing children's emotional needs. Many children grew up watching their parents struggling to make ends meet and continually worrying about their future.

Nurse Byrne kept busy working in the school system, witnessing the impact the depressed state was having on children. She knew children could survive poverty and depressed environments as she had experienced that during The Great Depression in the 1930s, but she seemed to know children needed more than food and water to survive. She was one of the few who seemed interested in how children were feeling. As you will see in the next chapter, it was rare to see someone in a position of authority in the schools being as attentive to children as Nurse Byrne.

During those times, it was not acceptable to focus on yourself, considered even selfish. Parenting styles were quite different than they are today as children were to 'be seen and not heard.' It was difficult to feel valued under those conditions. It was not just at home, but at school and church, the same rule applied. What does 'be seen but not heard'- mean to a child? If I see you, I do not want to hear from you. Pretend you do not exist - you are not relevant or worthy. It is saying to a child 'be invisible.' How do you think that feels to a child?

In the 1960s, children, raised to respect their elders, did not question them. Because of parenting styles and the views adults had about children, it was difficult for children to feel valued. This thinking affected their self- esteem, and many children struggled as a result.

The expectation was that children should do whatever adults tell them to do – no questions asked – no explanations needed; just do it because children did not need to know why. This thinking enabled some adults to say or do whatever they wanted to children. A lot of abuse and neglect took place in the 1960s, and no one did anything about it. Children punished or not believed if they talked about it, felt defeated and suffered in silence. Today things are much different as children are encouraged to come forward, listened to, understood, and protected from the ignorance of earlier times.

Uneducated parents, deprived of healthy childhoods, did not know the psychology of raising children. There were many alcoholic families, and many children raised in dysfunctional families. To be truthful, no one knew differently. The cycle went through many generations. The consequences of growing up during earlier times meant many people had poor self-esteem and had to figure out why, as an adult. Many people came from large families, with fathers who were absent because they worked long hours, were away working or struggling to find work to feed their families. Mothers had little time or energy to deal with their children's emotional needs. They spent endless hours doing household chores without the modern conveniences of today.

Many families were living in poverty. Nurse Byrne was aware of the challenges this presented for families. Knowing this, she took the time to get to know all of the children in her care and did what she could to help them. Many people did not realize she brought food to school for children who may be hungry. "Nurse Byrne would say to me, "Are you hungry?" and give me food. Maybe that is another reason why I went to see her. I was hungry, but you know, it was the whole thing. I needed her in my life." Student

Nurse Byrne, blessed to come from a positive, warm environment, knew what it was like to experience love and feel valued. Growing up, she learned her self-worth and the importance of self-love; perhaps that is why she appeared sensitive to those not so blessed. Many children got their first glimpse of self-value and self-love from Nurse Byrne. "She made each of us feel special in a time when there were so many of us that we rarely got one on one attention; that was her greatest attribute." Student

Many children in the Bay St. George area, raised in blue-collar households, had large families. My parents had ten children, and my father worked on the Ernest Harmon Air Force Base in Stephenville. I later learned we had plenty in comparison to many families as many fathers did not have a job, and most women were not working outside the home.

After the Base closed, my father, like many others, moved to Happy Valley-Goose Bay in Labrador to work. Our mothers, like Nurse Byrne, raised the children on their own. Fathers considered excellent providers, provided food and shelter, even if it meant you had to go away to work.

Being a good mother meant meals on the table and clothes washed. Mothers worked hard to ensure their children were fed, clothed, and cleaned. Those were the three factors that constituted being a 'good mother; the action of the love word demonstrated by what they did for you. However, while mothers were busy raising children, they had little time to interact with them. They scheduled all of their time to ensure the completion of their work as a 'good mother.' Unfortunately, the essential provision for emotional survival, to feel loved and wanted, was not there for many children.

My mother, like many others, had designated chores for each day of the week, and that did not change. Monday was washday, and it took up most of the day, as wringer washers were time-consuming as was hanging clothes on the line despite weather conditions. Dryers nonexistent meant clothes were hung on the line all year round, despite the harsh winters. My mother went into premature labor because she slipped on the ice while hanging clothes on the line. Life was difficult for women.

Nurse Byrne also took special care in washing clothes and even had a special technique for ensuring white blouses stayed white. According to Kathryn, her second oldest daughter, who was in awe of her mother's persistence to make things perfect, "Her clothesline reflected her perfectionism and the desire to do things the right way. She froze our white shirts to make them brighter as she always wanted us to look our best."

Tuesday was ironing day, which meant everything had to be pressed as line drying was not wrinkle-free, and 'permanent press' was a thing of the future. Everything ironed to perfection, from underwear to pillowcases, and as some may remember, bureau scarves were a trend at the time, and they too were made of cotton, which meant ironed. Nurse Byrne, known for her perfect ironing skills, pressed everything to perfection. "I was fascinated by how careful she was and how perfectly ironed the clothes were when she finished," said a childhood friend of the family who had the privilege of watching Nurse Byrne do her perfected pressing skill.

In our house, Wednesday was a baking day, and that meant about 20 loaves of bread, as it was a significant part of all meals. Nurse Byrne found time to bake and ensured her children had homemade bread and cookies made with love and care. I cannot remember the significance of Thursdays, perhaps more baking as bread did not go far in large households. Fridays, we had salt fish and potatoes (no meat on Fridays for religious reasons – Catholics did not eat meat on Fridays).

Saturday was cleaning day; clean the bathroom, scrub the floors, and polish the furniture. In most families, cleaning was 'girl's work,' only daughters had to help with household chores. Saturday was also bean night at our house (baked, boiled, or stewed). The style of beans was the only thing that varied from week to week; do not get me wrong, I loved bean night, and my mother was an extraordinary cook. Saturdays at the Byrne's house was spaghetti night. Kathryn expressively described their Saturday night meal. Her word choice reminded me that her Mother carefully chose her words, and it reflected in the speech of her children. "My Mom always made a beautiful pot of spaghetti with grated cheese. Our meals were as close to fine dining as you could get, with cloth napkins and home-cooked food prepared lovingly by our mom."

Nurse Byrne often used positive adjectives like 'beautiful' or 'lovely' when she spoke, demonstrating how she viewed life and how she presented it to her children (with an elegant and positive perspective placed on everything), even the simple things in life, like spaghetti. Kathryn made the spaghetti sound lovingly made and delicious. It is more of a feeling you get when you read or hear someone's words, which leaves an impression of their environment.

Our vocabulary is far more critical than most people realize. Words have the potential to enhance or destroy, so choose them wisely, and make it a habit to speak positively, using positive adjectives when you describe things, events, or people. If you have a vocabulary that consists of kind, loving, and positive words, it will affect your life. Imagine growing up in a household where you feel valued and loved. The words you speak influence the energy in your world. Referring to the power in one's words, "They can be used to sow seeds of destruction or germinate gorgeous, flowering experiences" (Choquette, 2005). We need to remember not to criticize or judge but to speak appreciatively, being grateful for everything, a lesson I was learning.

Sunday was a day of rest in Newfoundland and Labrador until 1998 when new legislation permitted Sunday shopping. When we were kids, the stores closed on Sundays, and most people did not work, but they did go to church. Our church had several masses on Sunday morning, and many of us kids sang in the choir. Denise, Nurse Byrne's youngest child, was in my choir. Sometimes we would have choir practice on Sunday's either before or after Mass or on Saturdays, lunchtime or after school. 'Practice makes perfect,' the norm in our catholic school system.

Nurse Byrne attended church with her children. They sat together as a family unless one or more of them were in the choir. I noticed those things because my father was away working, so we went to church on our own. We walked regardless of the weather conditions, as we did not own a car. I often wondered what it would be like to go to church as a family. I went with my younger brother and one or more of my sisters, and when my dad retired and came back home, we went with him.

I liked Sundays as it was the only day my mom played music on the record player. She seemed to relax a bit on Sundays. While we were at church, she cooked Sunday Dinner, which was a big meal we could not wait to eat when we got home from Mass. It was usually roast beef or baked chicken with vegetables and hot piping gravy. We could not eat or drink anything other than water before Mass as you had to fast at least an hour before receiving Holy Communion. We could not wait to get home for dinner. Sundays, we would get a special dessert. I am sharing this with you to help you understand the complexity of the roles mothers had, and yet Nurse Byrne was in church with her family and seemed so unconcerned, calm, kind, and so gentle. I noticed those things as a child because I could not help but notice her disposition. Nurse Byrne seemed to be everywhere. Never appearing frazzled, she cooked, cleaned, worked full-time, and still found time to be involved in her children's lives—both Mother and Father to her children and at most community events, one would wonder where she got her energy, as she did not seem to be short of any.

Mealtimes were important back then, but today, busy schedules seem to take priority over having a meal with family. Nurse Byrne ensured her family had food on the table and ate together as a family. It was not a question of whether or not you could make it; everyone expected to be home for supper, as suppertime was family time and a big deal in most homes. Mothers in the 1960s were adventurous cooks and took their roles seriously. Many collected cookbooks and experimented with foods from other countries. These were demonstrations of love and affection, wrapped up in things mothers did as their 'duty' to be a good mother.

Notable for her baking skills, "Nurse Byrne, made the best cookies" was a frequent statement made by those who had the pleasure of tasting her treats. Her demonstrations of love for her family would go beyond. She put extra effort into everything she did, such as creating a recipe book with a handwritten note addressed to each child, their spouses, and grandchildren. Yes, Nana Byrne put a significant effort into everything she did for her family.

Nurse Byrne saw all the kids in the schools as an extension of her own. Although she encouraged walking and fresh air, she sometimes drove her children to their activities, such as sports, choir, and endless swimming lessons. She also attended hockey games, soccer games, basketball games, and volleyball games. Everyone loved to see her at the school events. It was as if she was there for us, and in many ways, she was there for everyone. Most people remember her that way. She was a public health nurse; however, she spent so much time at our school that we believed she was our nurse, employed by our school. It was not until I was an adult that I found out the difference.

Nurse Byrne, present at every concert held by the school, and there were usually several each season, was a great lover of music, and living in Stephenville enabled her to get access to lots of entertainment. Music, valued in the school system, meant music teachers took their work seriously, tirelessly preparing children for concerts. Music teachers organized, directed the choirs, and often played the piano or the organ for masses and concerts. They also arranged music outside of the school. The Glee Club, under the direction of Jean Cormier, was the pride of the music community in Stephenville. Nurse Byrne was a member of the local glee club and sang at many concerts. She did not just go through the motions; she showed up for everything. She appeared to live life to the fullest and enjoyed herself while doing it.

My mom always said, 'there is no excuse for dirt,' and Nurse Byrne agreed as she carefully went through our hair with a fine-tooth comb looking for lice. Head-checks, no longer done in the schools, were a regular occurrence. Today it is the parent's responsibility, and most parents are working outside the home.

Nurse Byrne would comment on how clean we were and how

hard it must be for our mothers to keep us that way. Her way of checking in was to ask how often we bathed and washed our hair, and before done, ask how our mothers were coping. Nurse Byrne seemed very empathetic towards other women's challenges. Although she never mentioned her life, she always asked me how my mom was managing with my father away, even though she too was raising a family on her own. She had things so under control, that no one would notice any struggles or that she was quietly working to support her family, and unlike my father, her husband was not coming home.

Today, most women work outside the home while raising families; but we have microwaves, washing machines, dryers, and rumbas to vacuum the floor for us, and we have fewer children. We need to celebrate the women who raised families before modern conveniences. It certainly makes me grateful for what I have when I think of the old wringer washers and how it took women an entire day to wash and another whole day to iron. I know how busy my mom was so I am in awe of how Nurse Byrne did everything my mother did, worked full time as a Nurse, and as many people shared with me, she often would stop in and check on the sick and make house calls if someone needed her.

A young pregnant woman visiting her parents, scheduled to fly back home, started experiencing discomfort. Her mother, being worried about her daughter flying while pregnant, called Nurse Byrne. She quickly came to the house to check on her. People in the community knew they could rely on her.

One Saturday morning Nurse Byrne received a call from a young girl whose younger sister was sick, and their parents were away. She went to their house, cleaned up the child, and tucked her in. While the young girl slept, Nurse Byrne sat in a chair next to the bed in the room. When the child awoke hours later, Nurse Byrne, off-duty because it was Saturday, was still there. She did not seem concerned that she had spent several hours watching over someone else's sick child.

Nurse Byrne saw herself as responsible for all children and cared about their feelings. She even allowed a student's mother to come to her house to pick up medication for lice so that the child could avoid embarrassment at school. Nurse Byrne also checked in regularly with families who had lost one or both parents. These are not things she had to do, but things she chose to do. She was everyone's nurse, mother, and friend.

Life Lessons From The Field:

Soul Reflections: Love is a verb, an action word, be the love people are looking for in their lives. Do something special for those you care about by putting personal touches on gifts. Let your presence be a pleasant experience for others by paying attention to how you describe things, people, or events. If you use words like lovely, beautiful, and amazing, those things will appear in your world. Create a list of positive words and add to it daily. Allow your new vocabulary to influence how you see the world. Let us bring Sunday back as a family day, and if that does not work for you, devote designated time for your family. It is important to take time to rest and enjoy the quiet. Your mind and your body need one day of rest. Your family deserves it too. Life is meant to be shared with family and friends, and lived for the good of others. Join community groups, or volunteer your time to help others.

Soul Whispers

➢ Is there someone who needs you to see them or hear them?

➢ How can you make others feel uniquely special?

➢ Do you criticize or judge others?

➢ How do you describe your world?

➢ How can you enjoy Sundays with your family?

LESSON VII: FORGIVE

"Think of the people you know who give love in response to the negative energy directed their way. There aren't many people who respond lovingly in that situation. The ones who do can because they have love to give away."

~ Dr. Wayne Dyer

The truth will set you free, which is why I decided to tell my truth and forgive. Sometimes childhood experiences can leave us with feelings of fear, which may bring on anxiety. Living with anxiety can cause you to feel stressed and depressed. To free ourselves from this fear, we need to understand where it originates. Understanding requires you to go back to a place of love so you can forgive and move on.

We are all born with love, just watch a newborn baby. Unless there are underlying issues, babies are happy and carefree. They get lots of love and positive attention that make them feel important, and this feedback is the beginning of their self-confidence and self-esteem. However, sometimes life circumstances replace this self-love with fear, anger, and other negative emotions that can destroy your mental or physical health. When this happens, children grow up unsure of themselves, have little confidence, and often become unhappy and unsuccessful in life. I would like to discuss those particular life circumstances in this chapter.

Nurse Byrne was critical and memorable to many people because she stood out amidst the cold and often violent behavior we witnessed in school as a child. I hope people who suffer from childhood trauma are better able to understand the power we have as adults to move forward in our lives and heal from our painful experiences. The way to do this is through forgiveness. Forgiveness allows us to reconstruct images in our minds so we can stop memories of the past from being present and dictating our future. Choose to forgive and live in the present. Let your history be a learning experience to help you gain understanding, to improve your life.

Author Louise Hay reminds us that we cannot give what we do not have ourselves. It is important to acknowledge that not getting love at home is most likely because your parents did not receive love as a child. You cannot give what you do not have. Louise Hay tells us if we think our parents did not love us enough, we must forgive them, as it was not their fault. They were doing the best they could with what they knew at the time. This cycle continues until someone decides to change it. Let that someone be you.

To heal as an adult, you need to look at all the influences from your childhood. Once you understand these influences, you are better able to take responsibility for your life and forgive those who knowingly or unknowingly harmed you. Forgiveness is freedom. It helps you face the truth, and the truth will set you free.

Many of us owe our success in life to great teachers who encouraged us to further our education or follow our dreams. However, this was not the case for everyone—the education system of the 1960s and earlier operated under the same rules as the parenting system. Children were to be seen and not heard, making it impossible to have self-worth. No one knew about self-esteem or the importance of a good self-image, and it showed in the way many adults treated children.

Nurse Byrne treated children differently, which explains why they gravitated towards her. She expressed concern for how you were feeling and if everything was okay in your life. Her concern for the needs of children is why many others and I have great memories of her. With Nurse Byrne, I always felt seen and heard. I felt safe, valued, and respected. Mentally choosing to focus on love and kindness towards others is a powerful weapon to protect children who may be in pain.

"The warmth of her smile, her entire disposition told you that you were okay, especially in her eyes, and if she thought you were, then you must be, so you felt it too. It is a wonderful feeling." ~ Student

Abraham Maslow's Hierarchy of Needs, although developed in the 1940s, was not yet part of the philosophy of education in the 1960s. His theory states that until people meet their lower needs, they will not be motivated to strive for higher ones. Simply put, if you do not have food or water, it is unlikely you are going to do much else. It is simple and not difficult to understand or apply to children. Perhaps its application explains why we have breakfast programs in schools today, but we need far more than food and water to thrive.

Arranged hierarchically, we begin with physiological needs, but once we have those basic needs met, we strive for safety and security, which is protection from harm. Children look to adults to help them feel that way. When negative things, such as any form of abuse, happen to children, they need protection by the significant adults in their life so they can feel safe. Children who do not feel safe, live in fear.

When we leave home to begin school, we now have new socialization agents to shape and model our self-worth. If we are not getting what we needed at home, teachers can be the source of inspiration that motivates us to believe in ourselves, to go on to succeed. Just as teachers can become significant influencers in our life, Nurse Byrne became a considerable influence in mine.

When we feel safe and secure, we bond, focusing on our need for love and belonging to a family or group. If you do not feel safe at home, you might look for it at school. Nevertheless, what happens when you do not feel safe at school?

When you go to a catholic school, you belong to your parish, so your experiences at school become equally as crucial as your experiences at home. A child, fed and living in a positive family environment, is more likely to develop good self-esteem. Still, to value ourselves, we need to believe other significant adults in our life appreciate us. We get that message from how they treat us. Children treated with respect, learn to respect themselves and others.

During the 1960s, the schools prepared students for the workforce, treating us like assembly line workers, expecting to act and be alike. We dressed alike and lined up for everything. There was no place for uniqueness or individualization. We looked to school authorities to see how we should think and feel about ourselves. Meeting our needs makes us feel valued just as having our needs not satisfied makes it challenging and unlikely we will reach our highest potential. We have to believe we can before we are willing to try, perhaps why positive school environments are so optimal for learning. This chapter is important because, as you will see, Nurse Byrne helped fulfill many of the needs mentioned above for many children, and that is why those who knew her adore her. In many ways, she filled the gaps left by parents or teachers. To understand this, you need to understand what the reality of school was like for many of us. Let's begin with the philosophy of children.

There are three ways to view children: they are born good; they are born evil, or they are born neutral. The view you choose will influence the way you treat children.

The 'Bad' Kid

Children, starving for attention from the adults in their life, will do what it takes to get it. Children, not rewarded for good behavior, often resort to bad behavior to get the attention they crave. Keep in mind children were to be seen and not heard, so adults ignored good practices but did not let unwanted behavior go unnoticed.

Unwanted behavior meant kids are 'evil' or bad, and no one seemed to understand that bad behavior could be a symptom of anything other than the child being 'bad.' The churches preached we are born evil, and they baptize babies to get rid of the original sin. The philosophy that something or someone can hurt good children and make them act out, unheard of during those times. Children's behavior, often considered the outcome of being an evil child, left no room for exploration.

Over the years, I discovered while teaching Sociology of Families, that there was a historical belief that you had to beat the bad out of the child. Labeled as good or bad did not separate you from your action, it became your label, so while the 'bad kids' lived out their self-fulfilling prophecy, the 'good kids' got ignored, as most adults did not believe children were 'good or worthy.' Without reinforcement for good behavior, there is little motivation to do better. With self-love unheard of and self-worth a foreign concept, many children grew up with low self-esteem.

Believing kids were always up to something was the reason a priest kicked me out of the church when I was a child. Told to leave and not come back except for mass, left me confused as he said the church was no place for children to hang out. At the time, I was showing a child our beautiful old church and thought God would be happy to know I was there. I was not doing anything wrong in my mind. We were very quiet, and the child was in a stroller, so we were not running around. I remember feeling very confused by that incident. Raised to be respectful to my elders, I behaved accordingly, but no one could control what was in my mind. A few years later, the same priest, convicted of sexually assaulting children, left, and we never saw him again, which led me to wonder why we had to say, "Lord, I am not worthy." I felt resentful towards my church. Perhaps I did not understand why we were unworthy or what that meant. Children could never feel good about themselves repeating negative affirmations saying you are not worthy. The questions in my mind were endless.

I do not condone abuse or a church that protects abusers, but I do understand that abusers often were victims themselves. Everyone has to share the blame. Children expected to obey, no questions asked, had little regard shown to them for their feelings, would never be confident. They had to listen to all adults, not just their parents, and they were not allowed to tell anyone. Hence, a lot of abuse went undetected, and much of what we consider violations today were regular occurrences that no one talked about back then. Finding blame will not heal victims, acknowledging an ignorant society in need of change dictates our future. We learn from history, but we should not live it.

Today I preach that hurt people hurt people. Understanding this allows us to be empathetic and forgiving. It may be challenging to forgive those who hurt you as a child, but for your benefit, you must forgive and put it behind you. You cannot heal unless you forgive. Forgiveness is for your peace of mind, not for the person who wronged you. They most likely do not care or even remember you now. If you want to be healthy and happy, you must let go of the resentment.

Who Is Afraid Of The Small Letter 'A'

I began school in 1966, the same year the base closed, and my father left for work in Labrador. I was six and a half because we did not have kindergarten at that time. In primary school, hitting children was not just as a form of punishment but also as a method of teaching. The fear of ridicule or physical punishment was a deterrent to learning. This fear caused a lot of anxiety and sore stomachs but not a lot of education. I remember feeling teachers did not care about what we thought or how we felt. Children expected to learn while in fear of being hit, only learned how to avoid it.

I find it challenging to write this because I certainly do not want people to think all teachers were alike, but I need to express my experience to demonstrate the contrast of Nurse Byrne's actions toward children. In primary school, my only positive memory is going to music class as I loved it, and Jean Cormier made it a lot of fun. All my other memories are fear-based, except for my memories of Nurse Byrne.

In Grade One, the very first day of class, I remember some of the children cried when their mothers dropped them off. I walked to school with my sister, and it took us 20 minutes. I was glad to be there, so I sat there quietly, coloring in my new book. I was excited to be in school.

Once the mothers left, I noticed the teacher's disposition changed. She angrily told the children who were crying to stop and to sit quietly. She suggested that they color. I remember one little girl who cried uncontrollably didn't have a coloring book, so I tore a page out of my book and gave it to her with some crayons. The little girl stopped crying.

A few weeks later, a child had both of her hands slapped with a ruler because she did not make the small letter 'a' correctly. It appeared challenging, perhaps because we had never written on a blackboard before, and our little hands had not perfected writing with chalk. The teacher put the child over her knees and spanked her in front of the class because she would not stop crying. The little girl so traumatized, wet her pants, so the teacher made her stand at the front of the class in her wet clothes. She was humiliated, and I am sure it did not help her learn or like school. She just stood there crying while we stood in line to write our letters on the board.

It was very upsetting for all of us. I remember feeling horrified and afraid. Everyone was having difficulty writing the small letter 'a,' and we were even more scared after seeing what happened to students who previously weren't successful. I remember standing there, waiting in line, scared to death, praying I could make the small letter 'a' well enough to make the teacher happy. There was no way of being confident in your ability when you were afraid someone would hit you. Our teacher did not try to build self-confidence or self-esteem. Our only reward was avoidance, so we learned to lie, hide, or get someone else to do our work to avoid the strap. Had I known school would be like this, I probably would not have been so anxious to attend. I did not get slapped that day, but it wasn't long after.

I Thought We Were Supposed To Learn From Our Mistakes

Another day the teacher was walking around the classroom as we were doing practice sheets. She would pace up and down the aisles. I could hear the clicking of her heels as she walked slowly but with authority. The noise, repetitious, regularly paced, and loud amidst the quiet in the classroom let you know she was around. It was challenging to ignore, and I would be fearful when I knew she was nearing me. I hoped the sound would continue past me and not show signs of slowing down or stopping. I fought to concentrate on my work. When the noise stopped, the sound of my heart beating replaced it. I could hardly breathe. If she stopped, it meant someone made a mistake. I do not remember her ever stopping to say you are doing a great job. I was so terrified of her that I was unable to ignore her pacing, so I made a mistake.

We were doing an exercise where we had to draw a line between two identical items. The items were animals. I was checking over my work when I noticed I had connected one bird to two animals. I immediately began erasing one line to fix it. I was panicked as the clicking was coming from behind me. I knew the teacher was coming up my aisle. When she got to me, she asked what I was doing, so I told her about my mistake, and I was fixing it, but before I could finish what I was saying, she struck me across the head with her hand. My face was stinging, and I could hear ringing in my ears. I was so upset I started to cry. She angrily told me, "If you don't stop crying, I will give you something to cry about." That is my memory of my first year at school, and the next year wasn't much better. I wondered why going to school was such a big deal. I regretted my excitement and wished I were back home, watching Mr. Dressup.

❖ ❖ ❖

Separate The Boys From The Girls

At school, classes divided by sex until elementary school was the norm. Old school thinking meant girls distracted boys and vice versa. Teachers and principals also treated boys and girls differently. If boys were 'bad' (a commonly used word back then), they were placed in a girls' class for time out. Did this mean boys are 'bad' and 'girls' are good? As a child, I remember thinking that must be the case. I do not know if putting them in our class was to shame them, embarrass them or if it was because girls could teach them how to behave. Our teacher was strict, so maybe that played a role in the decision to put them in our classroom. She would discipline them.

One time a boy, while placed in our class because he was 'bad,' wrote on his desk with a pencil. The teacher took her leather strap from the desk drawer and started hitting him across the back with it. Sitting in the small student desk, not allowed to get out, he cried out in pain. The more he cried, the more she hit him. Horrified by what I was witnessing, I felt afraid that if I cried, she would hit me too. I had never seen anyone strapped before that day. I cannot imagine a child going through this today. He must have been traumatized, as I never forgot that incident, and remember it as if it were yesterday. I was seven years old at the time. I started feeling afraid for boys and began worrying about my younger brother as I was responsible for him. My fear led to concern, nervousness, and constant pain in my stomach.

Equal Rights ~ Girls Got It Too

I liked schoolwork, but I didn't like the anxiety I felt about school. I was sick a lot, and the doctor told my mother I had a nervous stomach. There was a lot of stress in my life for a small child, and a lot of it came from fear and negative emotions I was experiencing at school. I was a sensitive child, raised in a strict environment, and the school environment just made matters worse. I was very confused by the mixed messages of what I was learning in school and the treatment of students. I kept it all in during the day, but when I went to bed at night, I was a bundle of nerves. I worried myself sick.

In religion class one morning, we were told to line up in front of the class to show our homework, which was a drawing from a gospel story. I seem to recall Jesus and a couple of disciples but not much else in terms of detail. The teacher got the principal to come in to evaluate our drawings. The principal was a nun, and she carried a strap on her side. That morning I learned it was better to lie than be a young child drawing like a seven-year-old. Several of my girlfriends received the strap that morning. Their drawings were not good enough because the disciples' feet pointed in opposite directions.

The night before, I had asked my sister Irene who was in high school, to help me with my homework. I drew the picture, but I asked her to redo the feet as they were going in different directions. After she fixed the feet, I colored my image and put it in my bookbag. The next morning after strapping the girls, the principal used my drawing as an example of good work. I stood there feeling guilty for not telling them that I did not draw the feet. I was relieved for not being strapped, but I felt like I had let my classmates down. I felt ashamed and guilty. I had just lied, and that sin was on me regardless of why I lied. I later learned several classmates also got their older siblings to draw their picture because they were afraid, which possibly means those who got strapped never had older siblings.

The reason I share this is to demonstrate the importance of having someone like Nurse Byrne around. We needed her warmth and compassion far more than we needed her nursing skills.

She made all your fears disappear once you saw that warm smile and felt that caring hand on your shoulder; you knew nothing could hurt you. ~ Student

One of my former classmates told me that she remembered a girl being strapped for going to the washroom twice in one day. We were permitted to go once in the morning or afternoon, but not both. The rules were more about power and control than about anything else. They certainly caused a lot of anxiety for us as children, and I later discovered I was not the only one living in fear as a child.

Children Didn't Have A Voice, No Wonder I Got Laryngitis

My memories of primary school, the foundation of where our educational experience begins, were not ones of love and inspiration. In Grade Two, we were studying a book that had characters called Bossy Betty and Flossy Cow. I cannot remember the story, but the significance of the book to me is unforgettable. I vaguely remember my classmates talking about the book during recess and discussing who could play each character. One of my best friends at the time was much taller than I was, so I told her she would be perfect for the role of Flossy Cow because she was big like Flossy Cow. She, in turn, said to me, and you would make an ideal Bossy Betty because you are bossy. We were seven years old, so the conversation seems quite normal, and we laughed. There was no malice or intent to hurt anyone's feelings. However, that incident caused me the one thing in my life at the time that made me feel special and subsequently created many sleepless nights.

The schools, the church, the convent, and the post office all were within walking distance. Another student and I would go to the post office during recess time to pick up the mail and deliver it to the convent. I did not get snacks for recess as my mom cooked us a hot breakfast and lunch. When we would go to the convent, the sister who answered the door would often give us a treat. It would be a cookie, chocolate bar, or perhaps a dime, but she was most appreciative, and the job made me feel important. Sister Rosalie was my favorite because she always smiled and had kind words for us.

This one morning, while I was gone to deliver the mail, a student who had been part of the conversation about the characters in the book told the teacher I called my friend a big Flossy Cow. She did not tell her the whole conversation. When I returned, I was in trouble, and my punishment was losing my postal duties and awarding it to the student who had reported me. I was now 'the bad kid.' The teacher told the principal and other teachers, and they came into the classroom to talk to me and told me how bad I was and that I would go to hell. I remember going home and telling my mother one of my teachers told me I was going to hell, but parents had no authority over teachers, so as a child, you were always in the wrong. Being a catholic, I was so afraid of hell I was scared to go to sleep at night for fear I would die and go to hell. Punished for something I did not do, and not allowed to defend myself made me feel helpless. We were not permitted to clarify issues or explain ourselves, and we were to speak only when we were spoken to or given permission to speak. The teacher would never have told me I was going to hell had she known my side of the story. It is no wonder I got laryngitis that year. I felt like I did not have a voice, as the truth did not matter, so the message I was receiving was that I did not matter either

◆ ◆ ◆

Just Listen To Me, Please

I have some good memories of school, but it was in later grades. I had some great teachers who were encouraging and fair. Unfortunately, what stayed in my mind was the continued use of corporal punishment, especially for boys. As the years went by, I remember seeing boys thrown up against the wall, strapped, and scolded. In elementary school, a few boys and girls were carrying on before class. When the teacher walked in, they were playing catch with my pencil case. The teacher told three of the boys to go to the front of the room as he was going to strap them. Several of us girls were involved too, but the teacher only strapped boys. It bothered me so much that I stood up and said if you are going to strap them, you will have to strap me too. The teacher strapped three boys and me. I hated that the teacher strapped kids. I was willing to put myself in the line of fire because it bothered me that much. I was not trying to be a hero; I just wanted teachers to stop hitting boys. The leather strap was very painful. Today, its use is forbidden and considered abuse, but when I was in school, teachers could say or do whatever they wanted to kids.

You cannot believe you will amount to anything if you do not believe in yourself. How can you believe in yourself when you are feeling helpless and worthless? Nurse Byrne recognized this. She gave us love, respect, and acceptance. She knew success comes from an inner voice saying I believe in you, not from physical and emotional punishment.

Imagining Creates Reality

We had to become more loving towards ourselves by changing our thinking about ourselves despite our circumstances. Nurse Byrne conveyed that message to us by how she treated us. One of the things I remembered most was that she asked questions to us to encourage us to speak. Like soul whispers, her questions got you thinking about yourself. Her listening skills were exceptional, listening intently with a clear desire to understand. She never took her eyes off you while you were speaking. I always felt so good after talking to her. I felt heard, and that was a rare feeling. Nurse Byrne made you think what you had to say was important, and that meant you are too. She was the one positive memory that far exceeded the memories of fear and unworthiness dished out at school. This memory was not just mine but held by others as well.

> *"Her smile lit up the room - you felt it from the minute you entered the room. You felt good just being in her presence as she was welcoming and warm."* ~ Student

This is an accurate description of how Nurse Byrne made students feel, an excellent way to feel in comparison to the uncertainty we felt in the classroom. She was more than a school nurse for us.

◆ ◆ ◆

What Is A Guidance Counselor?

I asked Nurse Byrne if she was aware of how much kids loved her back in school. I told her that she was not only the favorite school nurse but also the person that many people looked up to for support. Her response made me think about how valuable Guidance Counselors are in the system today.

I was just doing my job. A lot was going on with kids that no one talked about, and it was challenging for them. I believe I was a good school nurse. I could see the children's needs. Very few people knew how much the children were in need. There were not any Guidance Counselors back then, so in some ways, I took on that role too. Most kids only want someone to listen to them. You do not have to do anything else.

I had not given it much thought before that day, but she was right. She was like a Guidance Counselor for us. There were not any Guidance Counselors in the primary schools at that time. The concept of a guidance counselor could not fit the model of a system that required children to -be seen but not hard. Guidance Counselors are a crucial part of our education system today. They are in primary schools right on up to high school. In the 21st century, we are aware kids have needs. On reflection, I am not sure it is fair to say that kids' issues are more significant today as when we were kids, we weren't allowed to talk about problems. I am sure problems have changed over time, but fundamental needs to be loved, to be valued, and to feel safe are still there.

"Her gentle and kind demeanor was a joy, like a breath of fresh air, "said one student. Yes, Nurse Byrne, your school visits were a welcomed interruption. You saw us, and you heard us. Being kind to others produces results. People are like magnets; we attract or detract from certain people based on how we feel in their company. Nurse Byrne had a force that drew people toward her. Ask anyone who waited in line-ups to see the school nurse. There is healing power in love and in how you make people feel when they are in your presence. You can intentionally bring love into someone's world just by thinking loving thoughts about them and acting on them. Nurse Byrne proved it. The energy of her presence was magical. "Her smile alone said you were okay. We could not wait for the announcement telling us the school nurses are here" students.

In 1968, the number of students kept growing. The introduction of kindergarten and baby boomers meant grade threes were put in a separate building on the base because the primary school couldn't accommodate such a large number of students. We shared this building with the 'integrated' protestant school; locked doors separated us. I do not know what grades were on the other side as we weren't allowed to go over there or to the left of the highest sliding board on the playground because it was not permitted. Ironically, being in a building that used to be part of an American Airforce Base, the protestant side was like enemy territory. Stay away or face the consequences of a trip to the principal's office. Some of us were brave enough to talk to our protestant friends while making sure we stayed on our side. I can remember being called to the office on more than one occasion because someone ratted me out.

I was like an outlaw because my friends were Protestants. The boys were a little braver and would dare each other to step over the imaginary line. Even as I write this, I cannot help but think about the hypocrisy. The different rules we had to abide by did not make sense when we were studying religion. My mother was a protestant until she changed her faith to marry my dad. Religion is not an issue in most Newfoundland homes today because we have public schools, but before the 1990s, it was a big deal. We didn't care about people's religion in our house. Half of my relatives were Anglican and the other half Catholic, but at school, it was different, so we had to sneak around our protestant friends. I resented the division religion created; it was one of the reasons why my Mom did not go to church. Even though she had changed her faith for my dad, she never felt welcome in our church. She felt like an outsider. I felt like I had to pick sides at school, but deep down, I never cared about the religious denomination of my friends, and neither did Nurse Byrne.

Nurse Byrne always concerned about perception and fairness, worried about how she made children feel. She did not cheer for her kids' sports teams in competitive sports because she was the nurse for all the schools, and regardless of religion, she did not want anyone to feel bad. Imagine attending your children's school events and staying neutral. "I was their nurse too, and come Monday morning; I didn't want them thinking I thought more of the children at St. Stephen's than at Integrated." I thought she was ours and was not sure I wanted to share her with the other schools. I was not the only person who felt this way, but she made us feel so special that we had no reason to think she worked at any other school.

Faith- based schools created more competition than anything else did and promoted a 'them and us' attitude. We all shared friendships outside our schools despite the divide the structure built. We were not supposed to associate with each other, but kids knew friends are friends regardless of religion.

Line-Up And Don't Cross The Floor

School nurses made regular visits to the school to maintain the health of children. There were so many children that it was necessary to have two and sometimes three nurses administering vaccinations and checking for head lice. There were anywhere between five and ten classes for each Grade in the catholic school, so line-ups became necessary to organize the nurses' visits. Most students were unconcerned about getting a needle if Nurse Byrne was the one giving it, so getting in her line was a big concern. Everyone wanted to be there because she made it as painless and pleasant as possible. Imagine those two words in the same sentence.

Once the announcement on the PA system said that the Nurses are here, teachers instructed students to proceed to the hallway and get in two straight lines. Students named the two lines as Nurse Byrne's Line and The Wrong Line. Every child would be standing there, wondering which path led to Nurse Byrne. Sometimes the lines were long, so you had no way of knowing if you were on the right track. Some people were brave enough to run to the front to see which line led to Nurse Byrne. They would then run back and tell the others. The students, who were in The Wrong Line, would look up and down the hallway to see if a teacher was around, and then they would quickly try to squeeze into Nurse Byrne's Line. If a teacher caught you, off to the principal's office you would go, and perhaps even strapped. The one thing about being caught was that you would not be allowed to get into Nurse Byrne's line.

Sometimes a student who was in The Wrong Line would push a student out of Nurse Byrne's Line. When a teacher would come by, they would say the student pushed them out of line. It was mandatory to stay in your designated line so the teacher would then make the students change lines. It was a game we all played in secret, but everyone knew about it, even the teachers. If you found yourself in The Wrong Line, it was like crossing the floor at the House of Assembly; no one likes to do it, but you have to do what you have to do. Although this may not be very complementary to the other nurses, it was not so much what they did or didn't do, as much as how Nurse Byrne did her job. In her loving way, she would ask you how you were feeling, listen intently, and give you your needle with a smile and a gentle touch. You were busy soaking up her charm before you realized she had already given you your vaccination. The warm gesture and motherly love you would receive once you were in her care made the price of being caught crossing the floor seem minuscule. The possibility of getting strapped was also a sacrifice and a reasonable trade-off just in case you made it to the front of Nurse Byrne's Line undetected. All we cared about was an opportunity to see Nurse Byrne. She did not judge us and treated us with respect. We needed this more than anything else.

You Can Go First

Another way Nurse Byrne made children feel cared for was through forward-thinking. She would anticipate what children were feeling and what she could do to alleviate their stress. As Nurse Byrne described to me, "There was nothing good about having to inflict pain on kids by sticking a needle into them. Sometimes planning by anticipating the needs of the children just made things easier for everyone." An example of a student's needs anticipated included Nurse Byrne letting students go to the front of the line if she knew they were extremely afraid of getting a needle. She did not want children embarrassed.

> *"Nurse Byrne was very gentle at giving needles. I was so scared that she often let me go first so that I did not wait and prolong my anxiety about getting the needle. I appreciated that she let me get it finished so that I could go back to class, and no one would see me crying." ~ Student*

Imagine finding this kind of love and consideration amidst the harsh classroom environment. Nurse Byrne seemed to have lots of love to give away. The love inside her was so plentiful that everyone who had the blessing of being in her presence received it. She did not let expressions of anger, shame, guilt, or fear be what she conveyed to the world, especially in the world of children. She must have known like attracts like so being angry at kids and strapping them wasn't going to make them behave or do better in school. The teachers who were hitting us were probably treated the same way as a child; maybe they were raised in criticism and condemnation.

It's hard to give what you haven't received yourself, so I choose to forgive them and set myself free. One of the lessons I learned from my negative experiences is that unfulfilled needs resulting from beliefs like 'be seen and not heard' can be used to motivate us. When we set ourselves free, we can take the negative experiences we had in life and turn it around. Sometimes negative experiences are in disguise to serve as a motivator toward our higher purpose. Many careers have come from a need to 'be seen and be heard' - Being a writer, educator, or speaker is an example. They all come from a need to be heard. When you decide to do something, despite what life throws your way, believe you will succeed, and you will as it's not what you do in life, but how you do it that makes the difference between success and failure.

Children have a lot to say if we take the time to listen to them. They will tell us what's going on in their minds, and it makes them feel valued. Listening to them with the intent to understand sends the message that they are worthy and that what they have to say is important. When we treat everyone as a unique and special individual, it increases self-confidence, self-value, and self-love. Nurse Byrne was a living example of the truth of this famous quote by Carl W. Buehner, "They may forget what you said — but they will never forget how you made them feel."

I learned from Nurse Byrne that when you love life, it loves you back. If loving-kindness is what you put out into the world, it is what you will attract back to you. It is the Law of Attraction kind of energy, and she seemed to have lots to give away. Thankfully, I was there to catch some.

Life Lessons From The Field

Soul Reflections: The truth will set you free. Forgive and forget because holding on to the pain will imprison you. History teaches us lessons we can learn and let go. Free yourself by learning from your past, not living from your past. We cannot control what happens to us in life, but we can control how we respond to it. Respond from a place of love and respect. First, love yourself and then take that love and offer it to others. Treat everyone as if she/he is the most important person in the world. Anticipate and understand their needs and take action.

Soul Whispers

➢Whom do you need to forgive?

➢Did you experience ridicule or criticism as a child?

➢How can you demonstrate forgiveness?

➢Are you allowing fear from your past to get in the way of your future?

➢Have you played your life small to fit in and make others like you?

LESSON VIII: LOVE YOURSELF

"What lies behind us and what lies before us are tiny matters compared to what lies within us."

~ Ralph Waldo Emerson

Self-love is not selfish; it is okay to love yourself. It is essential to love yourself if you are going to be happy and productive. We learn to love or not love ourselves from an early age. Our home-life shapes us into the person we become. We learn how we view ourselves through the eyes of our primary caregivers. Our self-image becomes a reflection of our world, so how we see ourselves is how we sell ourselves, an expression I coined to explain how we show up in the world. If we show up with self-love, we have a better chance of being successful and happy in all aspects of life. We establish appropriate boundaries and learn to value ourselves. We show others that they must treat us respectfully.

When shown love, we feel worthy and learn to love ourselves. Our approach to the world reflects confidence, making us more likely to succeed. However, when we are not shown love, we feel unworthy and have a lot of self-doubt. Our approach to the world will be one of criticism and fear, two major killers of many dreams.

Growing up in poverty or a large family in a small town makes it challenging to love yourself as people generally are competitive and in survival mode. People come together to support each other during hard times, but when someone is trying to better themselves, others often try to tear them down to make themselves feel better.

In the 1960s, your future dictated by your sex did not leave a lot of room for females to succeed in non-traditional roles. Boys would often go to college or take a trade, while girls were learning they might get to be more than a wife and mother. There was a lot of confusion and envy as women struggled to be liberated—introduced mainly to supportive jobs like clerical, healthcare, or hairdressing. Women often judged and criticized each other, making some women feel guilty for wanting to work outside the home. Women did not have many choices and often worked part-time in the service industry if they were married. Instead of supporting and encouraging success for women, it was often frowned upon and resented by people who stood back and said, "Who do you think you are?" There was always a shortage of work after the base closed; the main reason many locals left Stephenville; it was impossible to get a job. If you had a dream, you had to move to obtain it.

It took 50 years for me to learn that often, we are who we think we're not. Read that again, and you will understand why. Trying to keep yourself small to fit in only holds you back, one of the reasons many people growing up in small towns often never reach their full potential unless they leave. The struggle for self-love and good self-esteem continues as you take your small town self-image with you. Learning to compete with confidence takes time as you shake off your old thinking. It is challenging to grow as a person and gain the courage it takes to be yourself in a small town, perhaps why many never go back.

Local jobs are scarce, and many have to be underemployed if they return. Limited opportunity explains why there may be more people born and raised in Stephenville, living elsewhere. It is easy to identify by surname whether someone living in the town is part of the original families who settled there.

When I went to St. John's to see Nurse Byrne, she would often compliment me about how I looked or what I was wearing. One time she said to me, "Oh, you cut your hair. It looks nice." I had not had long hair in a very long time. Nevertheless, I just went along with her and said, "Yes, I needed a change." She was remembering me from when I was young. Often, her compliments were followed by, "If you think something nice about someone, you should tell him or her. You do not know if you will get the chance again. It is important to say nice things to people. My husband used to say that, so I try to live by that rule."

She was always teaching me lessons. Complementing people seemed to come naturally for Nurse Byrne, but sometimes there was a reason. Nurse Byrne lived intuitively and intentionally. She was a master at teaching self-love to us in the most natural way. Complimenting people was possibly part of her strategy to get you to feel good about yourself. What I did not realize that day was that I would learn more from Nurse Byrne than the feeling of giving or getting a compliment. I was about to learn about her intuitive awareness of other people. She seemed to be sensing something in me I was not aware of in myself. I always knew Nurse Byrne had a lot of empathy. There was that sense of 'I understand how you are feeling' about her. She had an awareness of other peoples' struggles and challenges. It was like she sensed how it might be affecting them. As one student described, " I remember how empathetic she was during my visits to the nurse's office. Knowing we had a large family, and times were tough, she would compliment me on how well I dressed, knowing how difficult it was for my mom to keep up with it all."

Growing up in a small town and in a large family often meant you put yourself last. There was not an acceptance of you thinking of yourself or wanting anything for yourself. Females expected to be selfless spent most of their time doing for others. Many girls grew up helping their mothers raise the children. Boys, left to their own accord, had minimal chores to do around the house. Self-Love was considered selfish, even self-absorbed. The consequence of this is you do not learn to love or value yourself or put yourself first, which may lead to a lot of unhappiness when you become an adult. Even self-care was unheard of until the 1980s. People think of large families as loving and caring like the Waltons, but the reality for many was more like the Jerry Springer show.

Nurse Byrne seemed to have an inner knowing she tapped into about how people were feeling. When I would visit her in St. John's, I would make sure I was in a reasonable frame of mind. I did not want to feel sad around Nurse Byrne or do anything to upset her. I am so grateful for each moment I had to share with her. I was there for her, not for me, and I kept that in mind. However, one day, she took me by surprise. In the middle of our conversation, she stopped speaking. She looked at me as if she had not seen me before and said, "You have a nice face." I thanked her and looked away. She reached out and carefully took my chin in her hands and began to examine my face as if she was looking for something. She said, "Look at your nose and your eyes." I told her my nose was crooked, as I had hit it off someone's head on the playground at school when I was a kid, and I may have fractured the bone because it was painful for a long time. She continued her examination in silence, giving no heed to what I had just said. Still holding on to my chin, she looked straight into my eyes and said, "Do you see what we do to ourselves? We go to our flaws instead of embracing what is good about us. I want you to go home, look in the mirror, and go through every feature on your face. Look for everything perfect. Do not look for any flaws."

Taken back, I started to wonder if she knew how I was feeling that day as I thought by now, I was good at hiding my true feelings. This experience made me think about the author, Louise Hay, and the mirror work she developed to help people learn self-love. Most of us find it challenging to look in the mirror, look ourselves in the eyes, and say positive things about ourselves. Nurse Byrne and Louise Hay both understood the importance of an exercise like this to help with self-love. I was in awe of the lesson Nurse Byrne had just taught me. She may have read Louise Hay's books on self- love, or maybe she knew that the mirror is an instrument to help us learn to be comfortable with ourselves. I tell people interested in personal development to begin with self-love, and the works of Louise Hay (Hay, 1984). It is easy to read and goes to the core of your being where you need to go to start your journey of self-awareness.

A mirror is a reflection of your inner self, how you feel about yourself, as well as your external image. It is a useful tool to help with self-love, which is like the first brick in building a foundation for mental and physical health, success, and happiness. We do not prosper without it. I had been studying this for a very long time, but Nurse Byrne caught me off guard and made me aware I had more to learn. She and I were sitting in the central area where others watch television or chat. Because it was quite noisy, we moved closer together so we could hear each other—the lesson we were doing forgotten as quickly as it had begun. Nurse Byrne asked me if I had any pictures of my family, so I took out my phone. She loved to look at pictures, and I had noticed during earlier visits looking at pictures helped her recall bits and pieces of her life and her children, so we spent the rest of the afternoon looking at photos on my phone and laughing.

We were like two best friends sharing our lives. She commented on every picture, especially the ones of my dog. She wondered what my dog was thinking in one photo, and we exchanged possibilities and laughed. She was enjoying herself, and that was important to me. She said she liked dogs, and her children loved animals and were always bringing home strays. When her children were young, they had a dog named Sir Humphrey Gilbert. Unusual name as Sir Humphrey Gilbert was an explorer who claimed St. John's for Queen Elizabeth I in the 1500s. I thought that was a great name and very sophisticated for a dog.

I enjoyed listening to Nurse Byrne and got a better feel for things she liked and had experienced in her lifetime. While looking through pictures, I noticed how she loved pretty things, especially clothes—that captured her eye for detail. While looking at photos, there was a wedding picture of my niece. Nurse Byrne carefully examined the dress. A two-piece outfit with a long-sleeved top and a flowing skirt was unlike any wedding dress she had seen before. Nurse Byrne looked at it carefully, admiring the dress and pointing out all its beautiful details. She then noticed the bride and said, "Oh my. Everything about her is pretty. The way she holds herself casually, she has to be casual enough that people will accept her." I thought to myself, how observant she was to have noticed that about the bride. All of a sudden, she became very conscious of her physical self. She asked me if she looked okay and adjusted her hair. I told her she looked beautiful.

Nurse Byrne became very self-conscious. The photo had made her aware of her appearance. Holding out her hands to show me her nails, she said, "I need my nails done." I asked her what color polish she liked and told her I would pick up some and come back tomorrow to do her nails. She looked surprised and asked, "You would do that for me?" I told her I would do anything for her. I was grateful for any opportunity to give back to her in some small way.

We had a fantastic afternoon, and after we said our goodbyes, I told her I would be back the following day to do her nails. When I was leaving, she called out to me just as I reached the doorway. She never spoke loudly as her gentleness extended into the tone of her voice, but I heard her amidst the noise. I went back and bent down in front of her. She looked at me and said, "You have no idea how much I enjoyed today. You made my day. I cannot thank you enough. I'll see you tomorrow." My heart melted. She had no idea how much she had made my day. My heart, filled with gratitude for every moment we shared, felt like it would explode.

I sat in my vehicle, trying to collect my thoughts. Aware that I need to learn to take a compliment and say thank you, I felt saddened. .I know that when you do, you are honoring the person who complimented you. I also learned I put myself down as a way of coping with my discomfort. Nurse Byrne had taught me what I had been teaching others, but I needed to learn myself; simple reminders of life lessons we know, but we do not apply in our lives.

I felt very emotional after that visit. I knew all the mothering I was getting from Nurse Byrne was perhaps something I needed at that point in my life. It was like she knew I was feeling bad about myself. I had a lot going on at that time, and my son was very ill. I was worried about him. I felt very alone. Even as adults, there are times when we need mothering. I was there for Nurse Byrne's benefit, but somehow, I still left her feeling better than I was because of the time I spent with her. Sitting there in my vehicle, I realized how much she reminded me of my mother, surreal to me, as these two women were nothing alike; however, as my mother aged, she had become more like Nurse Byrne, calm, loving, and caring. She had told me her biggest regret in life was that she never had time to enjoy her children when they were young. I understand better now as an adult. Nurse Byrne filled the void that many children had when we were young. I am grateful for the special day we shared, although it was an emotional visit for me. I am thankful for the realizations it brought me. I left determined to pay it forward by giving Nurse Byrne the loving-kindness she gave her entire life.

I went back the next day to do her nails and bring a few special chocolate treats, as I knew how much she loved chocolate. When I arrived, she did not remember me and was surprised to see me. I had prepared myself for this possibility. I took a deep breath, smiled at her, and just as if she were expecting me, I said, "I'm here to do your nails."

She seemed impressed, even excited that someone had come to do her nails. We chatted as I put on the clear polish she liked so much. She asked me questions about myself as if she was trying to get to know me, and I played along. When I finished her nails, she asked if she had to pay me. I said, "No, of course not. I would do anything for you." She then said, "I don't have any money, but I'm sure I can find some." We both laughed, and I told her she had given me far more in her lifetime than I could ever repay. She seemed pleased with that response even if she did not know what I meant by it. I knew, and that was good enough for me, as it made her smile and feel good about herself.

As adults, we appreciate great food and stability in our homes. We also know smiles, hugs, and kisses, and reinforcing self-esteem are important to our child's development. Sometimes parents are too busy to make this high on their priority list. For some, it may be about not being able to give what they have not received, especially if they do not understand the importance. The parents of children from the baby boom generation went from being babies to becoming little adults. They did not experience the freedom of running and playing. They did not know what it was like to be a teenager. Many did not receive affection from their parents. Survival, at the forefront of families, did not lend itself to children enjoying life; instead, they were expected to contribute to the household or moved on; a harsh reality for young people.

Lack of self-love affects relationships, whether they are social, work, or personal. You will always feel judged or criticized. If you had never received love as a child, you probably would not even know how to provide it as an adult. Cultivating relationships often result after time spent working on self- awareness, and often this happens after people experience a crisis in failed relationships or challenges with addictions. Love is like a hashtag for life. People search for it thinking they cannot be happy, healthy, or prosperous without it. What they do not know is that love comes from within, an excellent concept to learn at home or in school.

While interviewing for this book, I found a friend equally appreciative of receiving love and compassion from Nurse Byrne. He lives a soulful, spiritual life and, by his admission, is a better person today because of her. Eugene White, a former student from St. Stephen's School, shares his feelings about Nurse Byrne.

What a difference one person can make. She came into my life and changed everything! There are many great people in this world, but you rarely get the opportunity to experience their greatness personally. I believe we only get to meet someone like her once in our life; if we are fortunate. Nurse Byrne did not try to be unique; she just was, that was her. She affected so many people. Everyone learned from her, loved her, and had an 'experience' from her. It is amazing! A beautiful gift for sure.

Eugene shared a unique and funny story with me about an incident that happened when he was a child.

My New Best Friend The Boil

I think I was in love with her. In Grade 5, I remember going to St. Stephen's Elementary School in Stephenville, feeling like I was nothing. Being from Noel's Pond, (a small community on the outskirts of Stephenville), made going to school in Stephenville challenging. It was like people looked down on you because you weren't from town. We did not have much, so we felt like we were 'the low life' from Noel's Pond. As much as I hated going to school, the highlight of my day would be when I would get the opportunity to see Nurse Byrne. Getting a needle did not bother me; the reason for the visit was irrelevant; nothing seemed to matter when I got to see her. I do not know if, as a little boy of ten, whether I had a crush on her or whether her gentle way was appealing to me at that time in my life, but I couldn't seem to get enough of the love Nurse Byrne had to give.

I remember having what I believed was a boil on my neck. It was a red, swollen, painful bump under the skin on my neck. This Boil felt huge and stood out for the world to see like a stamp on my neck that said: "see poor kid even got an ugly red lump to prove it." It looked like an overgrown pimple. Looking at it was difficult. It was relatively large and caused severe pain, but nothing compared to the shame and embarrassment I felt about this ugly badge. I tried to keep it hidden under my shirt collar. I went to Nurse Byrne, and she lovingly cleaned it and bandaged it up. I felt so much better. She hugged me and reassured me that this strange lump was harmless and did not take away from my value as a person.

As I left her office that day, I was smiling from ear to ear, feeling so much better about myself and my new friend ~ the Boil. I went outside to the playground. I felt like a million dollars. I even began to feel grateful for this boil, as it had allowed me to get some of that 'feel-good medicine' Nurse Byrne seemed to possess.

The next day during recess, a couple of boys spied me on the playground and, as per usual, started wrestling with me. Getting picked on was a regular occurrence for me. All of a sudden, I felt this massive pain in my neck. My boil, my new-found friend, must have formed an abscess on my neck because not only was it painful, but a considerable pocket of pus started oozing out of it. I did not know whether to laugh or cry because my new friend scared the boys away, and off I went in pursuit of the help of Nurse Byrne. She cleaned it up and told me not to worry. She asked me if I was hungry and gave me a treat. It was common for her to provide me with little tokens of love, as she seemed to be concerned for my welfare.

She was the Sunshine in My Day. I can still see me going into that little room where she would be working. She would smile. Her smile lit up the room. She was 30 something years older than I was, and I was in love with her. However, as much I loved the attention of Nurse Byrne, I did not feel jealous knowing she had the same kind of love for every child who entered her office. This woman gleamed with endless love, so there was more than enough to go around. I knew when I left her office that day that I am special. No person or thing could take away the serving of self-esteem that Nurse Byrne had dished out to me.

I go back to her in my thoughts for everything. She is that One Great Person, the one I go back to and pinpoint where there was love brought into my life. I remember being in class, and the teacher would ask, "Okay, who needs to see the nurse?" I would raise my hand and say, "Me! I think I have lice." That was the highlight of my day. I did not have lice. I cannot even think of her as a woman, a mother, or a nurse. She is an entity, a gift from God. Her smile spoke to me.

I remember her as a humble person, very poised, one who kept her ego in check. I do not know what else I could say about her. I could die now, and I would be okay just for having been part of her life. Look at that woman's smile! How could you not love her? She was so beautiful. It is more of a feeling you get than something you can put in words.

◆ ◆ ◆

I thought to myself, what a wonderful thing to say about another human being. Imagine being such a great person, that someone would say that about you. Nurse Byrne influenced many people. Her goal was always to make people feel better, so they did, just for having been part of her life. Nurse Byrne taught us giving something as small as a cookie to someone hungry can have a lasting effect far beyond relieving hunger. When we do small acts of kindness, we are saying to that person that we value them. What makes someone truly 'special' is how they treat others. First, we need to love ourselves, and then we need to give that love to others. Let your actions show your worth. Choose to be the sunshine in someone's life.

Life Lessons From The Field

Soul Reflections: Self-love is not selfish-love. Self-love keeps us from sacrificing ourselves for others. It helps us establish appropriate boundaries so that others learn how to treat us with respect. Love comes from within, so do not look outside yourself for love. Remember this, 'So within so without.' You cannot love someone else if you do not love yourself. You cannot give what you do not possess. Look in the mirror and see your beauty, not your flaws. Do not criticize yourself or focus on what you do wrong. Always remember you are enough. Say, "I love and approve of myself, just as I am." If you say this enough, you will eventually believe it. Love yourself and others will love you too. Aim to be the sunshine in someone's day.

Soul Whispers

➤ Do you put others' needs ahead of your own?

➤ Do you say 'yes' when you want to say 'no'?

➤ Can you look in the mirror and say, I love you?

➤ How would you describe yourself?

➤ Do you demonstrate acts of love?

LESSON IX: BE THAT MEMORY

"Some days, I wish I could go back in life, not to change things, just to feel a few things twice."

~Source Unknown

Be the memory that changes a life. Imagine going through life and being unaware that your actions significantly influenced the wellbeing of another person. When you are memorable, you may become a life preserver.

Chris is a retired soldier who grew up in Corner Brook and would often visit his Aunt Sheila in Stephenville when he was a child. Her kind, gentle demeanor touched him. His personal story moved me in a very profound way. I felt how deeply impacted he was by his Aunt Sheila, and it made me consciously aware we sometimes unknowingly leave strong impressions on people. Think of the people you remember as a child. People most remembered are those who were kind to children. Imagine finding out that just being yourself resulted in you saving a life.

Just being in her presence was like a warm embrace, I couldn't wait to hear my father say, "Come on, Chris. Let's go to Stephenville." When I was a child, hearing those words made me so excited. My Dad didn't have to ask me twice as I loved to visit My Aunt Sheila. There was something about being in that house that just felt good. It was so clean, and her warm presence everywhere made the house feel like a home filled with genuine love. Aunt Sheila asked us if we were hungry, and before we could answer, she would have a cup of tea and a meal on the table. Her desire to give flowed naturally in everything she did and said.

Chris and I have never met in person, but over time, I came to know him and consider him a friend. It takes guts to share a personal story about your pain. I admire him for sharing and for taking the risk. Initially, unsure of his ability to tell his story, he figured he would be upfront about his challenges, so he sent me a message.

I have to be personal here. I suffer from Post Traumatic Stress Disorder. It's a result of my tours overseas with the military. It's a horrible affliction that has disrupted my life for more than 25 years. I want to share with you something Aunt Sheila has helped me with, without her ever knowing. I have traveled the world and have seen many things humans shouldn't see. I have witnessed the most unbelievable atrocities committed by other human beings that have made me question my faith in God and humanity. I know God is not responsible for what I have witnessed, but he is responsible for people like my Aunt Sheila.

Chris learned people like Nurse Byrne could significantly impact your ability to recover positive memories that give you strength, especially when you need it most. " For reasons I cannot explain, this lady, this person, who helped so many people in her life, gave me hope, just by her smile. In that smile, there is a healing power, compassion, and, most of all, there is love."

When Chris was in therapy, he learned how to replace his bad memories with good memories. The good memories would allow him to experience some good feelings, leaving him less stressed and better able to cope. People can dehypnotize themselves in much the same way Chris did in his therapy.

According to Maxwell Maltz, we go through life hypnotized by our real- life experiences (Maltz, 2001). If our experiences are harmful to us, we can lessen the effect by reclaiming positive memories. We can improve our lives and make ourselves more confident and successful, but we can also get rid of childhood or adult trauma. We are essentially getting rid of memories we don't want to keep because they make us feel bad, haunt us, or hold us back in life. These memories usually come from experiences that are so intense they leave lasting effects. When we replace bad memories, we are freeing ourselves. What happens in therapy is the patient becomes dehypnotized and released from the painful experience.

For Chris, by reprogramming himself to the memory of his Aunt Sheila, he was able to set himself free and live without fear associated with his experience. This strategy is not a permanent solution for PTSD, but like opening a door, it can allow you to walk through and experience new things. Perhaps over time, it may lessen the power of the triggers that bring on the attacks.

Chris shares his story to inspire others with PTSD to get help and relief from their suffering.

◆ ◆ ◆

There Is Healing Power In That Smile

My dad's name was William (everyone called him Bill). He was my best friend, and I was fortunate to have him in my life for a long time. I was born on Christmas morning at four minutes before ten. I was a whopping 14lbs 6 ounces, the last of seven kids. I wonder why! Growing up in a large family meant we did not have a lot of money, but we did have a lot of love.

At age 17, I joined the Canadian Armed Forces and served for 23 years. During that time, I met my wife, Tanya, in Germany. Her dad was a Canadian fighter pilot, so she was a dependent. From the first time I met her, I knew she would be my wife. I fell head over heels in love with this woman. She was 18, and I was 20. I didn't know at the time how special this woman was, and it was much later when I realized how blessed I was to have married such an extraordinary and loyal woman. We have been married for nearly 40 years and have two beautiful daughters who are the apples of my eye.

In 1993, just seven days after my first child Kassandra was born, I went overseas to the former Yugoslavia to carry out a tour with the Second Battalion Princess Patricia's Canadian Light Infantry under UN command. It was a very volatile time in this location as war ravaged the country. There were no good people in this conflict. I witnessed atrocities from all sides, things that still haunt me to this day! I will not go into the details, as I do not like talking about specific events. I would like nothing better than to forget them altogether. However, I can say it changed my life forever.

Upon return from the tour, I felt something was wrong. I could not sleep; I was having nightmares and feelings of unworthiness. This behavior was not me. I was the life of the party, and now I did not want to associate with anyone. I started isolating myself. I did not want to tell anyone how I felt as I was embarrassed, and I did not know what was going on with me. I was supposed to be this big tough person. I thought people would think I was weak or losing my mind.

I later learned this disorder has no eyes and can happen to anyone, big or small. My wife, with our beautiful new baby, caught off guard with my attitude and demeanor, made me ashamed of myself. I felt terrible about myself. She is the person most affected by my PTSD, something I live with and will go to my grave feeling shame and regret. No one knows what I have put her through over the years. I would start fights with her over the stupidest things, and she just accepted it. I never raised a hand to her, but my abusive mental assaults were worse, and yet she stayed with me and supported me every step of the way. She is an angel sent from heaven. There is no other explanation.

In 1994, a year after my return to Canada, I was posted to Valcartier, Quebec, to complete a one-year French course. The nightmares continued, and I was moody and depressed. Things were getting worse for me, and I wasn't dealing with it. My mom and dad came for a visit. They planned to spend two weeks with us and two weeks with my sister in Montreal. While visiting, it did not take long for my parents to notice something wasn't quite right. My father approached me and asked me if there was something wrong. Being the first person brave enough to question my behavior, he had no idea what was coming. I got outraged and told him not to ask me that question again. He walked away, and we did not speak about it again. It was quiet for the next two weeks as my parents tiptoed around me. They left to visit my sister in Montreal, knowing there was something seriously wrong with me. I had no idea what was to come or that I would never have the opportunity to apologize for my outburst. I was about to go over the edge.

One week after my parent's departure, my father suffered a massive heart attack and died. I was not strong enough to deal with losing him, and I could no longer hide what was happening to me. After his funeral, I somehow managed to finish my French course, even though our lives were still in turmoil, and the nightmares continued. Forced to face head-on what my father was trying to get me to acknowledge while he was alive, it took his death for me to finally hear what he had been trying to say when we last spoke. His death, a breaking point for me, made me acknowledge something wasn't quite right, but I rationalized that my father's passing exasperated the situation, so I still did not reach out for help.

The following year I was posted to Kingston, Ontario. I was excited about this opportunity. I thought a new place would be a fresh start for my family and me. It would be good to put everything behind me - but boy was I wrong. The nightmares came back and were more frequent and intense. I was still carrying on as if nothing was wrong, hoping it would go away.

I took a trip to Gagetown, New Brunswick for work, and on the drive back, I went through Trois Rivières, Quebec, where there was a pulp and paper mill. All of a sudden, the smell hit me, and everything started spinning out of control. I became overwhelmed and couldn't breathe. The odor from the mill was making me sick. It reminded me of all the human death piles we had to patrol past in sector north when I was overseas. The smell of rotting flesh, blood, and excrement was as strong as if I were still there. It wouldn't go away, and I felt like vomiting. It continued on and on. I was breathing heavily, and my heart was pounding through my chest. I was soaking wet, drenched with sweat. My first thought was I just had a heart attack, and because I was driving, I pulled over to the side of the road. When I did, the strangest thing happened; everything stopped. I remember thinking, "What the hell was that?"

I had many similar events after that; I was more scared than I had ever been in my life. This ongoing feeling of helplessness was taking its toll on me. As time went on, the attacks became more and more frequent, and each one felt worse. After each attack, I felt so exhausted and depressed that I wanted to lie down and die. I felt like I was sinking fast and didn't know how to save myself until one day I came home from work, and instead of going into the house, I sat on the front step and cried uncontrollably. I felt so helpless. I was so depressed and so sad. I didn't know why this was happening or why I was feeling this way. I didn't know what I was going to do, nor did I have any idea what was wrong with me. I didn't want to tell anyone because, at the time, I thought I was weak, and it's not a good thing to show weakness when you are in the military. I felt trapped inside my body. As I sat there sobbing, my two-year-old daughter Kassandra came out of the house and put her arms around me and said: "It's ok Daddy, it will be alright."

My heart melted, and I remembered the last time I had seen my Dad. I decided I could no longer care what anyone thought or said about me. I needed to get help so I could be the father Kassandra needed me to be. She deserved that much. I made a silent prayer for help, as my daughter, with her arms wrapped around my neck, wiped away the tears strolling down my cheeks. As she hugged me tighter, I said, "Kassie, everything will be alright. I promise you. I will be the best Daddy in the world for you." And I meant every word of it.

The next morning, I went to see a doctor on the base to find out what was wrong with me. In the back of my mind, I thought maybe I have cancer, and that scared me, but not as much as the possibility that something is mentally wrong. The doctor I saw had experience with mental disorders and trauma. We talked for a while, and he suggested I see a specialist at the National Defense Medical Centre in Ottawa for further examination. I did as he recommended, and the specialist had me complete a series of tests, and I had several appointments with two doctors.

The moment of truth came upon me when I went back to see my doctor for the results of my tests. I knew something wasn't right because both doctors were at the appointment. All I remember is one of them said, "You have PTSD, which is Post Traumatic Stress Disorder." I had never heard of PTSD, so I felt shocked and confused. I remember thinking, what is it, and why do I have it? I had so many questions. How long will this last? How do I get rid of it? As I continued asking questions, I knew there was more to come, as they weren't answering my questions and remained silent. The two doctors sat there and looked at each other, and then one finally said, "Well, it doesn't go away. It's something you will have to learn to live with." I was at a loss for words! If they had diagnosed me with cancer or some other disease, I would have known what I was dealing with, and at least hope of a cure. PTSD is here to stay, and it won't kill me, but I have to figure out how to live with it. It's not a death sentence but a life sentence with no hope of ever being released.

I continued treatment for several years but was not having much success. My first real breakthrough came in 1997. I was willing to do whatever it took to keep my promise to my daughter. I had been going to therapy for a few years, and one day something clicked. During one of my sessions, the therapist asked me a question that critically affected my life. He referenced my attitude and the connection between my perspective, my thoughts, and the way I feel about everything. The therapist was concerned about my negativity and the fact I seemed to feel negative about everything in my life. I have to admit I was in a doom and gloom way. I felt so helpless and not sure if things could get better. I was going on and on about how wrong everything is when the therapist stopped me. He looked me in the eye and said, "Given that you feel your life is so negative, and you think everything that happens to you is negative, is there anything or anyone in your past, before the military, that made you feel good? There has to be someone or something."

As if paralyzed, I stared at him, dumbfounded. Bells went off in my head as the face of my Aunt Sheila came to mind. She had the best homemade cookies. I could smell those fresh-baked cookies. I started talking about her. Everything about Aunt

Sheila was beautiful, including her home, which, tastefully decorated, had a place for everything. She was graceful in every way, from the way she spoke, walked, and the way she carried herself. Love just seemed to radiate from her. As a child, going to her house made me feel safe, as I knew this home was like a warm embrace. I can still see her standing in the doorway with a big, welcoming smile, and her arms wide open, just waiting for me to snuggle. She made me feel so loved that her warmth left a lingering feeling long after she released me. There was something special about her in every way. I loved listening to her speak as she had so much knowledge and seemed to know something about everything. She presented herself with so much dignity. Oh, how I loved my Aunt Sheila. She had the most beautiful smile. My dad would tease her and make her laugh, and when she laughed, it was a hearty laugh. I realized at that moment, 'yes,' there have been good times in my life. As the memories continued to flow, I felt excitement, just recalling how I felt going to Stephenville with my Dad to visit Aunt Sheila. I had that warm, happy feeling again. For the first time in a very long time, I smiled. Even my therapist smiled as he was excited that he had just witnessed a breakthrough.

As a child, I had so much love for Aunt Sheila. As a man, I remember how beautiful she was inside and out. It's no wonder she stayed in the hearts and minds of people for a very long time. That moment in time and those memories were the beginning of a new life for me. They opened me up, allowing me to experience good things in my life. I was able to move forward and look at life differently, and in the year 2000, I had one more reason to keep going back to those memories of my Aunt Sheila, as we had a second child. I have something many soldiers do not have, the support of a loving wife and children. They are my reason for being here today, still fighting to keep going.

I have seen the worst in humans, but I have seen the best in my Aunt Sheila. She personifies goodness in human beings. Aunt Sheila never knew what an important role she played in my life, but I know I am not the only life she has helped, and how important she is to others. I will always be grateful for my memories of her.

My name is Christopher Byrne. I am the son of William and Myrtle Byrne, the husband of Tanya Byrne, the father of Kassandra Ray Byrne and Rachel Erin Byrne. I live every day with PTSD. Every day I acknowledge it because if I do not, it will win. I will never let the bastard win. I hope this helps someone as it sure has helped me.

Kindest Regards,

Christopher Byrne

◆ ◆ ◆

Chris, having made a promise to his little girl that he would not give up, felt compelled to hang on for her and vowed never to let her down. Unfortunately, many people do not have the same motivation to keep fighting. I am grateful for Chris' breakthrough. I feel honored that he trusted his story with me to tell the world about his struggles and the hope he gained from the memories of his Aunt Sheila.

Chris taught me that as a soldier, the military comes first. Soldiers sign an agreement to serve their country, and that becomes the priority. Chris, like a broken soldier, felt betrayed for a long time. "It is like they own you, but when they see how broken you are, they don't want anything to do with you." He felt ridiculed, harassed, and bullied out of the military because of his symptoms, but he was not alone; many veterans who served their country suffered in silence or took their own life.

Chris, a pioneer for PTSD, held open the door for many who came after him. When he was experiencing symptoms of PTSD, the military had little if any supports in place to help soldiers coming back from war-torn countries. There was nothing in place because they did not understand how severe or how common PTSD is for veterans. Chris described it as fighting a war for the rest of your life. "We go to war for our country, but the battle doesn't end because PTSD never goes away."

Today Chris's story is far more common, but back in the 1990s, it was not something people knew much about. It is not surprising he had no understanding of this illness as it took many suicides of soldiers to bring PTSD to light and finally get the attention it needed.

In 2018, the Veteran Suicide Mortality Study measured the magnitude of suicide in the Canadian Armed Forces Veteran population by looking at suicides over four decades. (Veteran-Suicide Mortality Study 2018, 2020) Their findings showed that men and women veterans were significantly more likely to die by suicide than the general Canadian population.

In the 21st century, we know veterans who serve in war-torn countries are at risk for PTSD, and it is a precursor to suicidal thoughts and behavior. There is a lot more work done today to identify and help with this condition.

If you know someone suffering with PTSD please encourage them to seek help.

Life Lessons From The Field

Soul Reflections: Be the memory that changes a life; all you have to do is be kind, loving, and caring. Listen when people speak to you. Be the person they remember that made them feel great just for being in your presence.

Soul Whispers

➢ Do you welcome people when they come to visit?

➢ Do you create an atmosphere of acceptance in your presence?

➢ Does your home feel like a 'safe place' or a warm embrace?

➢ How would you like to be remembered?

➢ What can you do to make this happen?

PART III

- THE POWER OF LOVE -

LESSON X: BE A GREAT HUMAN BEING

"Cherish your yesterdays, dream your tomorrows and live your todays."

~ Source Unknown

To live your life as if it is your calling to be a great human being may be a tall order for some people; however, for others, it may seem to come naturally. Nurse Byrne, for instance, had only nice things to say about people, and that came naturally to her. One time when I visited her at Kenny's Pond, her daughter Kathryn was there. When she left, her mother said to me, "I do not have to worry about Kathryn because her husband is a fine man. Gerard is a sweetie, a wonderful man, very down to earth." Gerard had a special mutual bond with his mother-in-law and spent one-on-one time caring for her. Nurse Byrne told me she was as comfortable with him as if he were her son. Jessica is the daughter of Kathryn and Gerard. In this next story, she paints a picture of the love and connection she had with her grandmother. After reading her story, I am sure you will agree Nurse Byrne was not only a great human being but also an extraordinary grandmother.

My Gac

Some of my favorite memories of growing up in Newfoundland & Labrador involve my grandmother. I called her 'Gac,' so I will refer to her by that name in my story. There was not any significance to the name Gac other than the fact that when I was little, I was not able to say grandma or grandmother, so I guess that was my best attempt. The name stuck, and Gac did not mind that I had a special name for her that was mine alone.

"The Calling of my Soul" is a powerful and accurate title that reflects the colorful life of my Gac. She lived as if it were her calling to be this great human being. Everything she did was out of love; genuine, unconditional, and compassionate love. Everything about her reflected who she was, and this included her home and how she treated people when they were there. Her home was a place of comfort, just like her personality; it was a place of love. Going to her house was 'going home.' As soon as the car turned down O'Brien's Drive, I felt excitement as if I were almost 'home.'

My Gac put a lot of effort into being the greatest host. Her home was always welcoming. From the moment she greeted you, you knew you were in for a treat. She met you at the door and gave you this warm embrace before you entered her home. The way she held you felt like she was entrusting all of her love to you, and there was no rush to let go. I go back to the memory of her hugs to comfort myself. When I think of her, I treasure the memories of visiting her because I know how much effort she put into every visit. Those efforts made me feel special and loved. Gac did not do this just for me; she did this for everyone.

Gac would be thrilled knowing my friends and I were coming for lunch. I could not wait to bring them to her house, and they were equally excited when I'd invite them. We would walk from school to Gac's house, anticipating our lunch as if we were going to a special event. We knew we were going to have an extraordinary lunch that day, as Gac's lunches, never just thrown together, always were an occasion. Her sandwiches, made with fresh homemade bread, were specially cut and served with a presentation of fresh fruit, and of course, a home-baked dessert would top off the meal. Not only was her food delicious and made with love, the way she presented it to us at her table made the occasion even more special. Lunch was complete with cloth napkins and crystal glasses for our milk. It was a meal fit for a queen, and my friends were always blown away by her overwhelming hospitality. We got a warm embrace when we arrived and when we left. We walked back to school with our hearts and our tummies full, knowing we had just received the royal treatment, we couldn't wait for the next invitation.

Whenever a holiday or special occasion was coming up, Gac's house was the place to be. These times often brought the extended family together, with 12 or more people using one bathroom. No one seemed to care because that was a small sacrifice for a significant return. Gac made sure everyone was comfortable. The beds, made with fresh linen, had the coziest of sheets. Our favorite foods, waiting in the fridge, in the cupboards, or carefully placed on the counter. She even had a jar, filled to the brim with coins, sitting by the door in case the Dickey Dee Ice Cream Truck came down the street. She made sure we would not miss an opportunity to run after ice cream. It was as if she would think of everything. I loved our family gatherings because Gac made them enjoyable and memorable. She was the glue that kept her family together.

I will always be thankful for Gac's genuine loving personality. She not only anticipated our needs to ensure we had a great stay, but she let us know that looking after us was what she loved to do. Nothing seemed to be too much trouble for her as we enjoyed our stays and ensured that we knew she liked having us there.

I remember one particular day I wasn't feeling well. She wrapped me up in warm clothes and blankets and made a cozy bed for me outside on a lawn chair. She said fresh air cures everything. She was an outstanding nurse as it came naturally to her to care for those around her. I woke up on the lawn chair that day feeling much better, just as she said I would. My Gac knew how to make everything ok. The nurse in her was certainly her calling.

The care and love she gave us continued as we got older. Distance meant nothing to Gac. My parents and I moved to Calgary, Alberta, and Gac flew across the country to visit us. Of course, she would come bearing knitted sweaters and toques she had been working on for months before her visit. Gac also brought novelty items we couldn't get in Alberta, such as specialty subs and pizzas individually wrapped from Dominos Pizza House, and eclairs, cupcakes, and fresh bread from Danny's Bakery. Because these treats were custom made in small shops in Stephenville, they were not available elsewhere. She knew we would appreciate a little piece of home, so she would freeze it the night before her flight so it would be fresh when she arrived. While on her visits, she would often spend time at the rink watching me play hockey, and would follow it up with a foot rub. I will never forget the last time she did this, as it felt so good. Now that is love.

Hayz, my roommate at university, also benefited from Gac's kind gestures. We would often get a care package delivered to our door. The box stuffed with small items from the Stephenville Bulk Barn (jube-jubes, trail mix, mixed nuts, and chocolate almonds) left little room for her famous chocolate chip cookies, brownies, and banana bread. She individually wrapped each item and included handwritten notes on beautiful stationery in each one. It was like receiving a box filled with Christmas gifts. I knew she loved me, but reading those handwritten notes still touched my heart and confirmed her love for me.

My Gac had a special place in my heart and my life. She showed interest in whatever I was doing and made a special effort to encourage me by sharing my interests. Gac played floor hockey in the basement with me when I was barely seven years old. She held my sheet music while I played yet another new song on the saxophone (sounds painful even writing it ha-ha!). She made me feel special and important and encouraged me to try new things by getting involved in anything that interested me. My Gac was no ordinary grandmother.

I am grateful for her incomparable hugs. I am thankful for all the times I called her just to hear 'I love you, Jessica,' and most importantly, I am grateful for everything we shared; every meal, holiday, and walk along the beach. She created all those small moments into great memories. She helped me become who I am today.

Gac taught me life is a journey filled with experiences that help build character. Some of these experiences will test you, but it is during those times that your true self shows. She said always act responsibly and do right by others. Keep calm and act accordingly as your character is not defined by what you own or accomplish but by how you treat others in times of crisis.

Gac approached and conquered every event in her life with ease and grace. To understand the extent of her greatness, you only need to look at her life experiences. She was married at 29 and widowed with five children at age 37. A heart filled with love enabled her to become the best parent to her children and the best nurse in the community. The home she created for her children, filled with love, discipline, and spiritual guidance, was the place to be. She blessed her children with her wisdom and taught them to eat healthily, exercise, and always have an aching desire to help others. Providing more than most two-parent families could afford; she was a strong woman, bold, kind, fearless, and loving. She was an incredible role model that taught us how to be an exceptional friend, parent, grandparent, and nurse.

I am very proud and blessed to say this amazing woman was my Gac.

I cannot imagine my life without her. It will not be the same. Fortunately, for me, she has passed on her strength, resilience, and nurturing attributes to my mom (Kathryn). I benefit daily from her greatness and hope I, too, will inherit this genuine loving character, which inspires me to live as if it is my calling to be a great human being.

◆ ◆ ◆

Life Lessons From The Field

Soul Reflections: Live as if it is your calling to be a great human being. Express yourself by how you live your life. Do everything with love (genuine, unconditional, and compassionate love). Let everything about you reflect your greatness, including your home, and how you treat people when they are there. Treat everyone as if they are important and make every occasion a special occasion by using your best china, cloth napkins, and best silverware. Never miss an opportunity to make someone feel special. Write handwritten notes on beautiful stationery; include them in packages, send them by mail, or, better yet, hand-deliver them. I guarantee they will feel the love. Life will hand you events that will test you, and during those times, your character is defined by how you respond and how you do good for others. Choose to act, not react.

Soul Whispers

➤ How would you define a 'great human being'?

➤ What would it take you to become that person?

➤ Do you demonstrate love through your actions?

➤ How can you ensure that no one misses the ice-cream truck?

➤ How do you respond to undesirable situations?

LESSON XI: DON'T CHEESE PIZZA THIS

"Feeling is the one and only medium through which ideas are conveyed to the subconscious. Therefore, the (wo)man who does not control (her) his feeling may easily impress the subconscious with undesirable states."

~ Neville Goddard

It is extremely important to focus on what you want, not what you don't want. The principle law of the universe is The Law of Attraction, which says we attract what we think, how we feel, and who we are; in other words, what we focus on grows. If you tend to focus on negative thoughts, it should be no surprise to you that the whole world seems negative to you. People who feel like nothing good ever happens to them may not realize that by changing how they feel, they will change their outcome. They can change how they feel by changing their thinking.

We have control over how we see the world, subsequently influencing what we bring into it. A better life begins with a better thought. When people describe you as a kind, loving person, that is most likely your experience in the world. Nurse Byrne is a case in point. To obtain the results she received, she must have focused mostly on what she wished to accomplish in the world. Otherwise, her outcome would not have been the one she desired.

Keep in mind the universe always delivers. It is also important to recognize the universe does not have a filter, so it responds to what you think about whether you want it or not. Some say it has no sense of humor, so it does not seem to understand negative words like' no or not,' so talking about what you do not want will bring you more of what you do not want. Worrying is a great example. Worrying is like praying for something to happen that you do not want to happen. Why? Because you are focusing on what you do not wish to happen, and 'what you think about, you bring about,' you need to be mindful of your thinking. If you are feeling bad, pay attention to your thoughts and change them. Otherwise, you are allowing yourself to feel bad. When we feel bad, we are attracting more of the same.

Recently, I learned a new phrase ~ 'Don't Cheese Pizza This'~ which is a catchy way of saying 'stop focusing on what you don't want to happen.' If we waste a lot of time worrying about simple things that may never happen, this concentration can cause what we worry about, to happen. While what we focus on grows, what we resist persists, as it is still concentrated energy. This next story will help you understand this concept as it teaches you when you have a bad feeling, making a little adjustment will impact the outcome, and 'don't cheese pizza this,' will make more sense to you.

'Don't Cheese Pizza This' came about as a result of a story told to me by Maureen, Nurse Byrne's daughter. Later I discovered she had misquoted the phrase, but I found it so catchy, I decided to keep it. The original catchphrase from the story was 'don't mini-pizza this,' which has the same meaning, which will become clear to you once you read the story.

◆ ◆ ◆

Courtney, a friend of Nurse Byrne's granddaughter Claire, tried to teach her friend to apply the law of attraction to a situation that was causing her to worry needlessly. In other words, she was worried about something that had not happened yet. Worrying is future thinking. What we think about, we bring about!

As a child, Claire liked visiting her grandmother. She would soak up all the love and hospitality that her grandmother gave while inhaling the fresh- baked goodies. Claire is the daughter of Anne Marie, Nurse Byrne's firstborn child. Claire grew up on the other side of the island, but after high school chose to go to Grenfell College in Corner Brook, about an hour from where her Nana Byrne lived. She visited her grandmother every other weekend, bringing along her laundry and sometimes a friend or two. Nana did not mind.

When Claire telephoned Nana to tell her she and Courtney were coming for a visit, Nana Byrne was excited and thought, and I will surprise them and get them mini pizzas from The Pizza House. She knew Claire was vegetarian. She thought about the many debates they had about the topic, agreeing to disagree about the benefits of being vegetarian. Nana Byrne thought pizza would be a great compromise, and Dominos was always a special treat for her family. However, Claire had other thoughts,

Everyone Loves Domino's Pizza

Our whole family was obsessed with mini pizzas from Domino's Pizza House. Every time we went to visit Nana Byrne in Stephenville, we would order a case of mini pizzas to take back home. When I became a vegetarian, my grandmother insisted it was not a good thing to do. She believed God put animals in this world for us to eat. She was also concerned about the challenges of proper nutrition, as she did not think a vegetarian diet was a healthy way to eat. We had many debates about it. When I decided to give up dairy, I was now pushing that conversation to a place she was not willing to go. Nana did not understand anyone wanting to do that voluntarily.

On Easter weekend, my friend Courtney and I went to Nana Byrne's. I did not want to leave Courtney alone during the holiday weekend as her family lived in New Brunswick. Excited to spend the weekend at Nana Byrnes, Courtney joyfully came along. She knew this would be no ordinary weekend as Nana Byrne's hospitality was no secret. All my friends knew she put a lot of time and effort into every detail to make her visitors feel welcome.

Courtney and I were about to take the exit to Stephenville when I called Nana Byrne to let her know we would soon be there. She told me that she had picked up mini pizzas from Dominos, and will put them in the oven now so they will be hot when we arrive. When I hung up the phone, I let out a big sigh. Courtney said, "What's wrong now." I told her Nana Byrne had ordered pizza, and I went on a rant. Now it is going to be this big thing – Nana Byrne went out of her way to do something special, but I don't eat dairy anymore, she knows this. We are going to have the same conversation, and I am going to hurt her feelings. It will be a big thing. She refuses to understand why I won't eat dairy. Courtney listened to me go on and on, and then she turned to me and said, "I think that is the most negative thing I have ever heard you say. Why walk into this situation looking for that outcome. You will channel it into your life and manifest cheese on that pizza. " I knew she was right, but I also felt this was an impossible situation.

Claire continued to talk about the possibility there would be cheese on the pizza. She told Courtney how Nana usually dismissed the conversation because she did not believe anyone should stop eating dairy unless they had an allergy or intolerance to it. Claire did not want to hurt Nana's feelings, so despite being urged by Courtney just to call Nana and say 'no cheese on the pizza, please.'

Claire continued whining about the cheese dilemma and became more and more stressed. Her constant whining and refusal to do something about it began to annoy her friend, who could tell Claire was not going to give this up. Finally, Courtney had had enough and shouted at Claire, "For the love of God, would you stop Cheese Pizza-ing this."

They looked at each other and busted out laughing. Courtney continued to explain to Claire that she was going to manifest cheese on the pizza if she did not stop worrying about it. Knowing the Law of Attraction and the principles of manifestation, Claire agreed she was indeed setting herself up for failure, so she gave it a rest and changed her thoughts to a true vegetarian pizza without cheese.

When they arrived in Stephenville, the first thing they noticed when entering the house was the aroma of pizza cooking. Nana was in the back of the house and had not heard them come in. Claire looked at Courtney and rolled her eyes, and quickly ran to the stove. She opened the oven door to sneak a peek at the pizza before Nana got to the kitchen. "I took a deep breath and set my intention to let go of all my preconceived negative thoughts about what I assumed was going to happen. There in the oven were my mini pizzas: all veggies, no cheese." Claire looked at Courtney with a big grin. Nana Byrne had been one step ahead of her, and the smile on Claire's face let Courtney know the manifestation process was a success.

After hearing this story from Maureen, "Don't Cheese Pizza This" is what comes to mind whenever I hear someone anticipating an undesired outcome of a future event. A simple reminder to focus only on what you want, can change your life. More importantly, never underestimate the actions of a grandmother. Nurse Byrne anticipated the needs of others to make everyone happy, and as a result, she created positive outcomes. She knew better than to put cheese where it did not belong.

As for Claire, she learned a lesson, "I can honestly say that moment changed the way I look at things. I think the phrase "don't cheese pizza this" all the time when I am hoping for the best outcome or heading into a stressful situation. I have "cheese pizza'd" not running out of gas, pulling off significant events at work, and my partner not forgetting to pick up almond milk at the grocery store on the way home. It has taught me to stop looking for the worst in people and situations, and as a result, I am less stressed and happier. I no longer assume worst-case scenarios I cook up in my head for no valid reason."

Note: Domino's Pizza in Stephenville is original and can only be purchased there.

Life Lessons From The Field

Soul Reflections: Focus on what you want, not what you don't want. Deliberately choose your thoughts. Positive thoughts bring positive feelings. Being around positive people brings positive energy. Your point of attraction comes from your power. Change your feeling, change your life. Don't be a Negative Nellie. Bring joy and pizza wherever you go.

Soul Whispers

➤Are you a worrier?

➤Do you spend time thinking about what you don't want?

➤What would you like to manifest in your life?

➤Have you tried changing a negative thought to a positive one?

➤Do you believe you are the creator of your own experience?

LESSON XII: BELIEVE

"The lovers of life are the healers of life because they're the believers of life."

~ Sonia Choquette

You must believe it to receive it. It takes a burning desire and faith to ensure we get what we want in life. As the author, Dr. Wayne Dyer used to say, "You won't see it until you believe it." This next story will demonstrate how Nurse Byrne was able to manifest a trip to Buckingham Palace. She fulfilled her wish by focusing on her desire and believing it would come true. When we follow the principles of manifestation, intentionally or unintentionally, we bring our desires to life.

In the late 1970s, Nurse Byrne began to experience the empty nest syndrome as her last child, Denise, went to university. As much as she liked to keep busy with community events, she also liked quiet time at home reading, baking, or relaxing in a hot bath. Nurse Byrne had a lot to be grateful for as her children had all done well. She had come to accept the fact she did not have her husband to share her retirement.

Nurse Byrne was fascinated with the Royal Family. Even though she had not been to Europe, she admired the eloquence of

Queen Elizabeth II and loved to read stories and look at pictures of her in magazines. I was not surprised to learn this as Nurse Byrne, often described as graceful like the Queen, had a touch of class that made you feel you were in the presence of royalty. I guess one could say she was a combination of Grace Kelly and Queen Elizabeth with the heart of Mother Teresa.

There was an English flair in many aspects of Sheila's life. England had claimed Newfoundland long before it joined Canada in 1949, so the British influence is present in the architecture of many old buildings throughout Newfoundland. Sheila's maiden name was Smith and her ancestors from England. The house she grew up in had most of its furnishings brought over from the old country. Perhaps her exquisite tastes came from British influence.

As much as Sheila loved to read about the monarchy, she had not given much thought to going to see Buckingham Palace until 1984 when she received several postcards in the mail from her youngest child Denise.

Traveling throughout Europe with a few friends, Denise had been studying at the Harlow Campus in England. When she completed her internship, she and a few of her friends stayed on to discover the wonders of Europe. Denise sent her Mother postcards from all the places she visited and shared with her the important details of her adventures. Her description of her travels and the scenery in the European countries sounded beautiful to her mother. It made her visualize her daughter's journey. She began to dream about one day visiting all the wonderful places she had only seen in magazines.

Sheila received her first postcard from Ibiza, an island in the Mediterranean Sea.

May 29, 1984, ~ Ibiza, Spain

Hola Madre,

I'm here in Ibiza. The weather is muggy and hot. We are recuperating from yesterday's sunburn. It is beautiful here. I'm sitting out on the terrace writing you, and there are Spanish children playing with a ball down below. I finally get to see real palm trees. Beautiful! Estupendo! I wish you were here. This postcard shows a typical scene in this part of Ibiza; the cobblestone steps very worn, and the people poor. There is a swimming pool next door to us that we use, but we live on the beach of the Mediterranean Sea.
Take Care. I love you.
Adios, Denise

Sheila found herself reading and rereading the postcard. She continued doing this several times a day as it brought such joy to her heart. Each time she read it, she smiled as she could feel the heat of the warm Mediterranean air and hear the children laughing as they played in the courtyard. Sheila could hear the wind and the sound of ocean waves in the distance. She pictured the bright sun sparkling on the water. She smiled, thinking of how much she loved the beach, hot sun, and warm breezy air. Sheila whispered to herself, "One day," as she smiled at the thought of the great trip she envisioned. She gently placed the postcard on the fireplace mantel and said aloud, "Denise, you and I will make this trip together."

A short while later, Sheila received a second postcard from Denise. This time it was from Paris, France.

July 27, 1984, ~ Paris, France

Bonjour Mama,

I'm here! I can't believe it! The city is beautiful! Everything I thought it would be. We have spent a few days here, and now we are on our way to Lyon (France) and then on to Switzerland. The four of us are doing great. The more, the safer. Don't worry, Mom. We all take good care of each other. The French bread here is delicious. The city is quite busy. It's lovely to see, hard to shop in.

I got your spoon. Love you, Mom. Yes, I'll be careful.

Love Again.

Denise, in Paris. xoxo

According to author Catherine Ponder, "What you radiate outward in your thoughts, feelings, mental pictures, and words, you attract into your life affairs" (Ponder, 2011). Unbeknownst to Denise, her mother was visioning Paris, the shops, the beautiful cafes, and the hustle and bustle of the city. Sheila could hear violins playing while people with their perfect French accents asked for loaves of freshly baked bread. She inhaled as she imagined the smell of freshly baked bread with butter melting deep into every slice. She found herself thinking about the countryside, the towering trees, endless beaches, and the mystery of foreign languages.

Denise kept sending postcards, and her mother kept visualizing. Every word Sheila Byrne read took her one step closer to her dream as she continued to imagine all the sights and sounds her daughter described enthusiastically in her writing. The seeds now planted, the beginning of the manifestation process had begun.

When Denise returned home at the end of the summer, her mother, bursting with excitement, could not wait to tell her about the idea of going to Europe. "I want to see Buckingham Palace and to go to all the beautiful countries you have seen. I know I was not interested in going to Europe before, but after reading your postcards, it sounds so marvelous. I would like to go there one day, and I hope you will be my tour guide. That would be so lovely, don't you think?" Sheila could hardly contain her excitement, which made her daughter laugh. Denise smiled and assured her mother that one day they would go to Europe together, and she would love to be her tour guide.

They talked about Denise's adventures in detail for months after her return. Denise looked forward to the day she and her mother would board a plane and travel Europe together. She did not know about her mother's visioning or her continuous reading of the postcards daily. Both of these activities, being part of the manifestation process, attracted the European trip at just the right time. Diving timing is always part of a higher plan.

In September of 1994, Denise and her husband Todd took her mother on a European Tour. It would be the trip of a lifetime, a dream come true, something Sheila Byrne had been visualizing for ten years, and now it was a reality.

As Denise described the trip for me, I could only imagine what it must have been like to share this experience with her Mother. Every daughter should take a trip with her mother to see the world through her eyes, just the way a mother experiences life with her children. Their vacation reminds me that we all need to take a step back from our busy lives and experience the world with those we love. The memories become an incredible gift to share with others.

I hope you will be encouraged to plan an adventure with your mother or someone special. It does not have to be Europe or somewhere exotic. It can be anywhere. The 'where' doesn't matter; it is the 'who' that counts. Let Denise's story be your inspiration.

Take Me To See The Queen

Mom was fascinated by The Royal Family, so we took her to Buckingham Palace in London. She was elated and couldn't believe she was there as she loved to read about the Royal Family, and now it was so real to her. We went to Venice, Italy, where we shared a Gondola ride (a traditional, flat-bottomed Venetian rowing boat) across the Grand Canal. The Gondola Driver wore a navy white striped shirt and a straw hat with a red ribbon wrapped around it, such sweet memories for us all. We then went to Rome to see the Sistine Chapel in the Apostolic Palace, the official residence of the pope, in Vatican City. Mom being a devoted catholic, was in awe of the chapel and the great works of Michelangelo.

We also went to Lucerne in Switzerland, where we saw the famous Chapel Bridge and took a drive through the Black Forest, a mountainous region in southwest Germany, bordering France, and then we took a Rhine River Cruise.

In Paris, we went to see the Eiffel Tower, The Louvre, and the Notre Dame Cathedral. To satisfy Mom's taste for chocolate, we took her to Brussels in Belgian, where we enjoyed the finest chocolates in the world. I still remember us buying several boxes. They were the most delicious chocolates I had ever eaten. We couldn't get enough of them, and while walking through the streets of Brussels, we suddenly realized we had eaten an entire box. It was a taste like no other.

We also went to Monaco on the French Riviera in Western Europe where we visited The Prince's Palace, the official residence of the Prince of Monaco. Mom's highlight was walking barefoot in the sea as she enjoyed the ocean and sandy beaches more than anything in the world.

Mom purchased souvenirs for her children and grandchildren from every place she visited. It was a trip fit for a queen and a once in a lifetime experience; just talking about it brings back sweet memories for Todd and me. I will cherish them forever.

After the tour, we took a train to Scotland to visit with my sister Maureen. Todd and I stayed for a few days and flew back home while Mom visited with Maureen and Rod for a few weeks. The food, the fun, and the laughter made Mom hungry for more travel, so after that trip, we spent one Christmas in Venezuela and another in the Dominican. Mom loved the warm weather and ocean views, and it was a great break from the harsh Newfoundland winters. She also wanted to see all of Canada, so we took a train ride from Ottawa, Ontario to Vancouver, British Columbia, and from there, we flew to Calgary, Alberta to visit with Kathryn and her family. For Mom, her entire life revolved around her family.

◆ ◆ ◆

After hearing Denise's rendition of their travels, I found myself longing for a European tour to visit the magnificent historical cities that are home to the greatest stories in European history. I learned if you want something bad enough, you must keep it fresh in your mind. If you can imagine it, you can obtain it.

Nurse Byrne focused on her dream. She believed in her trip for ten years. She proved you can attract what you want into your life, as long as you don't give up. Knowing this means you need to keep your thoughts pleasant, harmonious, and happy; because what you think about, you bring about.

If you have a desire to take a trip or to travel to a different part of the world, picture yourself doing it and hang on to that thought because you never know, perhaps like Nurse Byrne, you may wake up one day and find yourself there.

Life Lessons From The Field

Soul Reflections: We attract what we think about, but more importantly, we attract who we are. If we are kind and loving, we will attract kind and loving people, events, and experiences into our life. We cannot attract what we are not. If you wish to experience good things in life, you must be a good person. It is simple. The universe is always listening and always responds. You must be grateful for what you have and what is to come. You must believe it to receive it. Be careful -where- you think about, as you just might end up there.

Soul Whispers

➢Is there something you wish to experience with a special someone?

➢What can you do to manifest that experience?

➢Do you monitor your thoughts?

➢Do you pay attention to how you are feeling?

➢Do you feel gratitude every day of your life?

LESSON XIII: LET GO AND LET GOD

"Life is not a struggle but a surrender."

~Neville Goddard

Let go and let God. It will lighten your load. As much as I wanted Nurse Byrne to hold this book in her hands, I now realize if I had published it, I would have had to let her go. Not prepared to do that,
I hung on until she let go first. Because of my fear of letting go, I was in a holding pattern. I did not have closure for the book because part of me was still afraid. Now I realize that in her passing, Nurse Byrne was permitting me to finish the book.

When Maureen messaged me that her mother had passed, it was as if she was saying to me, "it's time." I had heard that before, in 2002, when my oldest brother Mel called me early one morning and said, "It's time." He did not say anything else, and I replied, "Okay," and hung up the phone. I knew what I had to do. I had to take my four-year-old son and drive across the island to let go of my father. Those words, "it's time," have no other meaning to me than 'letting go.' Filled with fear, anxiety, pain, and panic when my brother said those words to me, I quietly did what I had to do and drove in silence to Stephenville.

After reading Maureen's message, I sat quietly on the couch in my sunroom, collecting my thoughts. I heard the words, "It's time," but this time, the voice was inside my head. It was the voice of Nurse Byrne telling me, "Okay, it's time. Finish the book." In her kind, gentle manner, she reassured me I now had her permission. My fear of publishing the book was my fear of letting go of her. I knew what I had to do ~ pack up and go to Stephenville to let her go. Once again, filled with fear, anxiety, pain, and panic, I quietly did what I had to do and drove in silence to Stephenville.

The night before, Maureen had sent me a message asking me to say something at her mother's Wake, so while driving, I thought about Nurse Byrne and what I would like to say about her. My only memory of a Wake is a priest or nun leading the rosary, and the only person who speaks is the priest. Roman Catholics are ritualistic, slow to step outside the rules, but I guess things have changed. I am sure Nurse Byrne would be happy about that because she was very open-minded. I did not know if the Wake for Nurse Byrne would have a rosary, but for some reason, I could hear her voice in my head saying, "It's time to change it up a bit anyway." I had to say enough about Nurse Byrne to remind people of her greatness while keeping it brief.

I had so much to say, but I kept thinking about how challenging it will be for me not to say too much.

When I arrived in Stephenville, instead of pulling into the driveway, I decided to park on the other side of my parent's house. I reached back and grabbed my purse to put my phone in it. All the while, I was looking down. When I opened the door to my van just as I looked up, a moose ran by. I almost hit the moose with the door, as I had not seen it coming. I was shocked and realized how close the moose had come to physically trampling me; that would have left me a great story had I survived it. The moose did not seem to notice how close it came to running into my vehicle. It was out of its territory as the house was not near a wooded area. It may have been confused.

Ironically, a moose had also shown up in our yard when my mom died. There had to be a connection. I could not help but wonder if there was some significance to this moose showing up because I had learned that animals are spiritual messengers. I teach a course in Indigenous studies, and there is a common theme that animals appearing out of nowhere are bringing an important message from the spirit world. I do not believe in coincidences, so I decided to look it up to see what spiritual message this moose may be bringing. It said,

> *If a moose shows up, it means you can feel proud of your recent accomplishment and share it enthusiastically with others, not to be boastful or competitive, but for the simple joy of sharing (Farmer, 2006).*

My initial thought, finish the book! Share it with the world and stop second-guessing yourself; that is the message from the spirit of the moose. I now had confirmation and a reminder of why I was writing the book in the first place.

◆ ◆ ◆

I decided to go to the funeral home for the afternoon 'viewing' to say hello and pay my respects. When I went inside, I felt a sense of Deja Vu as I remembered the feeling I had in 2012 when my mother had passed. It is a feeling that is hard to let go of as the connection to your mother is undeniable, and we have that same connection with our children. The continuous contact between mother and child is perhaps why a mother's lineage is so important in many aboriginal cultures regardless of the sex of the child.

I often think the mother-child relationship is powerful because of the umbilical cord. A broken link causes tremendous pain, as the bond between mother and child becomes severed. The cutting of the umbilical cord only physically releases us to the world; it does not disconnect us psychologically or spiritually from our mothers. Connected to our mothers for life, the real pain of the severance takes place when one or the other leaves this world.

I knew how Nurse Byrne's children felt as I had experienced that pain. I hope, in time, they realize that death does not end the relationship; it changes it. Following the grieving process, I experienced a continued awareness and connection with my mother that I never had when she was living. I feel like she is always with me now, but when she was alive, we lived in separate towns. In many ways, I feel closer to her, as I continuously feel her presence.

As expected, there were many people in the funeral home. I saw Nurse Byrne's children, grandchildren, and many of her friends, including retired teachers, and relatives of her husband. I remember looking around and wondering what they had done with her. I could not see the casket, so I thought she was in another room because there were so many people. Maureen came over to say hello, so I asked her where her mother was resting. She instantly said, "Now, you don't think Sheila Byrne is going to rest in a casket, do you? Cremation was her choice, so we fulfilled her wishes. Mom, well prepared, planned her funeral, naming those who would read, sing, and take part. Some of the original people have passed while others couldn't make it, but with minor adjustments, we are fulfilling her wishes."

Maureen pointed to a box on a table across the room and continued, "Michael made a beautiful wooden box to put her ashes in. We will put messages in it before we bury her on Saturday next to our Dad in Corner Brook. We took her to the beach last night, so a piece of her will always be there."

I later found out a sprinkle of her ended up in a lot of her favorite places as her children had taken her on tour the night before to the special locations where they had shared memories. I shook my head and grinned as I could picture the family talking to their mother at each site. All I could think was 'how cool is that,' and I felt her smile.

The House That Michael Built

I walked over to the beautiful wooden box sitting on display and stared at it. Processing everything Maureen had just said, I felt like it had to finish uploading into my brain. It all seemed surreal. Nurse Byrne, cremated and leaving a piece of her soul at the beach at Port Harmon. It made me smile as I thought, "I would like that too. There are a lot of us who have special feelings for that spot." I made a silent wish that our souls meet up one day by the benches on the beach.

I turned my attention to the beautiful wooden box that sat on the table. As I looked at it, I thought how difficult it must have been for Michael to build this. I could only imagine his thoughts while crafting the most important thing he had ever made in his life. It must have been an emotional but yet satisfying thing to do. At that moment, I remembered Nurse Byrne telling me Michael had built a house for her. On several occasions, she said to me that Michael had promised he would build her a home, and he did. She would then note how comfortable it is and asked me if I liked it. She was referring to the long-term care facility she was living in at the time, but she would beam with pride. Each time she told me that story, she repeated it word for word, always so proud to tell me the story of the house that Michael built.

Sometimes I wondered if she confused her memories of her father, her husband, and her son, but one thing was for sure, she loved them and had a special relationship with each of them. I could not help but think they were like the holy trinity for her. She always smiled and spoke with such pride when she spoke of either of them. Many times, she used their names interchangeably. I never corrected her and just basked in the joy she was feeling at the time. Often when she mentioned her father or her husband she would say, "Every woman deserves a good man. My father was a good man, my husband was a good man, and my son is a good man. I wish every woman had a man as good as my husband. He was a fine man."

I smiled, thinking of the memory she shared about the special men in her life. As I stood there admiring this beautiful wooden box that housed the ashes of the greatest woman I had ever known, I wondered if this was the house referred to in our conversations. It was perhaps the most important house a son could build for his mother. She would have been proud to know he did that for her and certainly would have told me about it. As I stood there, I imagined that the perfectly crafted house in which she now rests is very appropriate as her final resting place.

◆ ◆ ◆

Da Dementia

I first heard 'da dementia' at a symposium on aging from a woman sharing the story of her family's experience with dementia. She and her family had moved back to Newfoundland and into the family home to care for her aging mother. The story was unique as her mother had been a nun, and her father, a priest. My first thoughts were what a great story to write, but as I listened to the romantic tale, I soon realized this story had a dramatic twist. What began as two Catholics leaving their 'calling' to become a family, became the story of a family leaving their life to become caregivers to an aging woman, (a widow, ex-nun, mother, mother-in-law, and grandmother) with dementia. I listened carefully to the presentation as my mind drifted back and forth between Nurse Byrne and my maternal grandmother, who had lived with us during my childhood. Dementia had become the enemy of the soul for both of these women. Dementia was a familiar story in my family as we had faced it several times with close relatives. When I was in my early twenties, I did a field placement at the senior's home in Stephenville Crossing. It ended up being the same place that my sister later worked, and where my grandmother took her last breath. What affected me more than anything was watching families admit their loved ones. It was very sad, especially if the loved one did not want to go but had to for their safety. I still remember the guilt, shame, and worry my mother experienced when she brought my grandmother there. It was a very painful experience for her. When Nurse Byrne's family made the difficult decision to place their mother in care for her safety, all those memories resurfaced for me, and I wanted to help because I understood it.

Although the presentation was informative, it was also a heartfelt story told creatively with humor and love. I could not help but think what a great way to discuss an otherwise painful reality of a disease that comes like a thief in the night and robs a family of memories. As the speaker shared her story, it became clear to me that this amazing experience wasn't about theft but a blessing bestowed upon a family. I was learning to perceive dementia as a gift. This woman expressed gratitude for the opportunity it gave her children to create intentional memories with a grandmother, who otherwise they would not have known. This new way to view dementia made me sit up straight and listen intently.

Like a sitcom, the chaotic story of three generations living in one house with young children and an older woman quickly losing her independence played out in front of us. Every episode was funny, painful, or an unbelievable learning experience, describing the realities of living in a rural community with a lack of services and products this city family had previously taken for granted. Finding alternative methods and products or learning to do without were some of the challenges the family faced. It had all the makings of a great reality show. The family hung on to every moment, their entire experience sounded like an adventure they had booked online. Each family member had a role to play. The lead characters were the mother and daughter, with her husband and two young children playing supportive roles in 'Da Dementia' series. In my mind, I pictured children sitting on the bed, asking endless questions as they watched their mother feed her mother. I thought about the gratitude the children will feel when they are older and can fully appreciate these special moments.

The story of this family intrigued me. The journey they were on, planned by God, seemed like a blessing given to a family who under different circumstances would not have had the opportunity to share their lives. The presentation was a brilliant way to share an otherwise painful story. I found myself smiling as I recalled many great memories of my grandmother and her dementia. Time heals the pain and kills the chaos, and when things settle, the memories created during that time are treasures to be shared and retold for generations to come.

It's been nearly 40 years since Grammie's diagnosis of dementia, and I have memories of her thinking she was still living at our house. I would help her look for things I knew were not there but in her mind. Those memories are sweet now. For many years, she spent her time knitting a blanket for a baby who had already grown into a young boy of 8 or 9 years old, but we never told her as she unraveled that blanket and reknit it for several years.

I would not trade those memories. As much as we loved our grandmother, when she finally passed, the memories we shared the most were those after her diagnosis. I feel blessed to have shared those times with her. We had her because my grandfather was lost in the woods and died. It resulted in my grandmother coming to live with us. We were grateful as we did not have grandparents, and we would never have known her otherwise as she lived on the other side of the island. I did not feel robbed of our relationship because of her dementia. It was more like a different chapter in a book. I had not thought about that experience until I listened to the talk about Da Dementia, and I felt grateful for being reminded of the blessing an illness can bring.

Sharing precious time with someone who is vulnerable and needs you is a blessing. Failing health makes you weak, and having a family to help you during this critical time in your life is a gift, as is being able to care for a parent, a privilege denied many. Knowing everything in life can be a crisis or a blessing reminds me that life is how we see it, a lesson my mother shared on her deathbed. Some people can sacrifice their life to care for another person, but most people are not able to do this for a variety of reasons. This story was intriguing because it is uncommon for a family to be able to do what this family did, and then, to share their experience to help others is priceless.

◆ ◆ ◆

When I think of Nurse Byrne's children, I think of their pain. I know they felt helpless and a lot of anxiety about their mother, but in time, they will find comfort in their memories of time spent with her. Watching their mother, a significant woman, loved by everyone, trapped and held captive by her failing body seemed unfair. She lived a healthy lifestyle and spent her time doing good in the world. Looking for justification will not change anything, but learning to let go through acceptance of what we cannot change, and finding gratitude for the blessings, will surely bring peace.

Sometimes while we are in the midst of an experience, we can only feel the pain of the experience. The pain of a loved one falling ill challenges us in the same way that the pain of death destroys us. We grieve in both situations as they leave us feeling helpless and deeply saddened. When the healing begins, we become open to seeing the blessings of the shared experience. Our memories become beautiful and comforting. The pain remains but subsides as we start to acknowledge our gratitude for having shared this experience with our loved one. We come to understand that closure is a gift wrapped in time spent with our loved ones during their illness or on their deathbed. Not everyone receives this gift. Sudden death or daily living can deprive us of this precious blessing.

Kathryn, Nurse Byrne's second-oldest daughter, and I talked on the phone several times in the last year before her mother passed. Like Maureen, Denise, and Michael, she found it extremely difficult living away from her mother and tried to get home as often as possible. The worry of having an aging parent, especially one with dementia, is extremely difficult for families. It is emotionally exhausting, and the guilt and sadness of missing a parent can sometimes feel more than you can bear. When we have a loved one with a terminal illness, we often feel like we have lost them long before they pass. As Katherine expressed to me,

> *Sometimes, it is beyond painful. I live at a distance, so I try to call my mom every day, but some days, she does not even know I phoned her. Sometimes she thinks she is at her parent's home in Harbour Breton, and I remind her that she is at Kenny's Pond in St. John's. I love her lucid moments, but then in a flash, she is gone. I feel like my mother is my best friend. She always had my back, and I never doubted that she loved me. She is, indeed, the best thing that ever happened to me. I feel blessed to have had her for a mother. I thank God for her each day. Now I feel her slipping away from us, and it hurts to see a vibrant,*

strong, loving woman who cared for everyone, so vulnerable and timid.

When someone passes, those left behind cling to the memories of the time they shared with their loved one. There is a lot of healing in those memories. Kathryn recalled her memories of their mother and the joy she brought to their lives. In her stories, we get a glimpse of an amazing mother who intentionally created incredible memories for her family, reminding us, "Your body cannot heal without play. Your mind cannot heal without laughter, and your soul cannot heal without joy," Catherine Fenwick.

◆ ◆ ◆

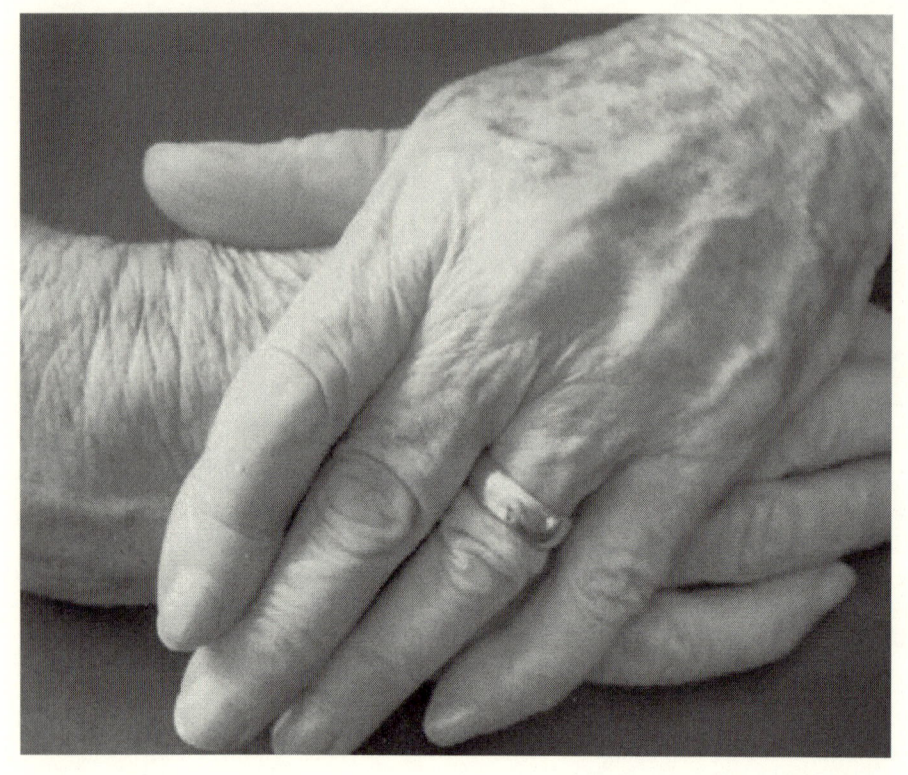

Photo by Aiden Mahoney

Healing Hands ~ Healing Hearts

Life With Mom

Growing Up Our Home Was Our Sanctuary.

It was warm and inviting. Mom bought an abundance of wood and fire logs for the fireplace in our living room. We spent a lot of family time in that room amongst the warmth and love that our mother gave to our family. When we were not enjoying a fire indoors, we were enjoying one outdoors in our backyard. Sitting around the fire, we shared food and laughter. We had many great times at home, enjoying each other as a family. When Mom started to get dementia, and we had to sell the family home, it was very difficult for all of us. Our house, where we shared so much love and laughter, was a symbol of who we were as a family. It was our home, a memory of our mother's strength holding on to it after our father had passed. It was as if we were letting go of our father, our mother, and our family. Mom had kept it going for us. It was always about us being happy, healthy, and loved. Selling the house was like letting it all slip away.

Mom Never Missed An Occasion To Celebrate Or To Keep Our Father's Memory Alive For Us.

On Valentine's Day, she decorated our windows with valentine hearts cut out of lace, and she gave each of us an individually wrapped heart-shaped chocolate. Pancake Day, we had homemade pancakes with little trinkets hidden inside. On Halloween, we had a carved pumpkin, and she did up unique individual bags of goodies for every kid on O'Brien's Drive. She made every occasion special, but Christmas was extra special at our house. She was a perfectionist, so the tree was done just so. She loved to have the house decorated, so we all helped her. My dad loved extraordinary things. He used to get treats for us for Christmas when he worked on the base, and when he passed, my Mom ordered them special for us to carry on the tradition. Throughout the year, she would keep the supply in a chest, and at Christmas time, she would put them on a tray for us to enjoy. There were boxes of the finest chocolates, every flavor you could think of, and there were several types of candy, including toffee and ribbon candies. After Maureen moved to the UK, she contributed special chocolate and nuts to replenish what we had previously enjoyed. Mom also ordered hickory farm cheese. My Dad used to love it, so we grew to love it too. Thanks to our Mom, we always kept a piece of Dad with us, in all our family traditions.

Mom Had A Special Relationship With Each Of Us.

Mom treated each person in our family special. She believed

in uniqueness and individuality. Even her cookies, made with love, carefully selected for each child, their spouses, and the grandchildren. Mom created a special family cookbook and included the recipes of all our favorite cookies, Coconut Cream, Chocolate Chip, and Coconut Drops, to name a few. In the book, she did a special devotion to each of us and wrote it next to our favorite cookie. Her personalized message, like an award, was a memory to treasure. She gave each of us a copy of the book. Everything she did was special, unique, and done with love.

Life With Mom Was An Adventure.

When we were little, mom would pack a lunch, the six of us with our dog Humphrey would get in the car, and off we would go to one of the several local beaches. We would enjoy a swim, hanging out at the beach, and a great picnic. When it rained, we went to the local indoor swimming pool. On occasion, we enjoyed a hotel stay with a pool, and we would go to A&W, which had a drive-in (carhop) where they would come up to the window and serve you. That was a massive treat for us, and one of the few times, we ate junk food. Mom made everything fun and perfect because she cared so much. She took us to PEI, Nova Scotia, and St. John's. She was so brave going off on her own with us kids and the dog. She had only just learned to drive, but she was fearless. Determined her children would never feel deprived of anything life had to offer, she made sure we had as good as or better than any two-parent family.

Our Vacations Became Staycations Because Of Her.

It is no wonder after we were married with families of our own that we went to Mom's house for our vacations. Her home was like a resort, except she treated us better. There was not a thing we wanted that she did not provide; all the food we could eat and plenty of toys and activities for the children. Each grandchild was important to her. She treated each one special, and they knew their grandmother loved and valued them. Even as they grew older, they could not wait to go to Nana Byrnes. We had a houseful of people sharing one washroom, but we did not care. We made it work because it was so much fun. One of our favorite memories is going to Black Bank to swim, lie in the sun, and enjoy a family picnic. We never went anywhere else for vacations because we did not want to be anywhere else but home, where our mother resided, and our memories of growing up still lingered in our minds. Why would we not want our children to experience this kind of love?

Life Was Good Because Of Mom.

When my dad died, I felt sad, but I felt even sadder for my mother. His death had an impact on her and each one of us in a different way. The children ranged in age from two to eight, so us older ones have some memories of life with Dad. Each of us had a different relationship with our Mother. I am sure this is true for most families. Mom's ultimate goal was to love us and care for us as best as she could. The more she did for us, the more I wanted to give back to her; because she deserved it. When I think of her, I do not know how she did it; how she raised five kids with little support. Mom never worked in the summer because she wanted to spend it with us. She worked hard her entire life and retired when she was 65. She taught us everything she could about life and gave us the best experience humanly possible.

She Made Everything Seem Effortless.

Everything was so free with mom. She had an energy about her that just made everyone feel loved and cared for, and nothing seemed to be an inconvenience for her. Everything seemed to flow perfectly without disruptions, just the way she liked it. She was a natural caregiver and loving person who worked endlessly to give us the best life possible.

How Can We Say Good-Bye To The Person Who Made Life So Perfect For Us?

I do not know how life can go on without her, but perhaps we have to do what she did for us after my Dad passed. We can hang on to the memories and keep her traditions alive. We can act on the wisdom she instilled in us. We can go on living by giving our love to each other as brothers and sisters and husbands and wives. We can love our children, nieces, and nephews and ensure they never forget the love their grandmother had for them. I am sure they will also miss her. Together we will share our memories of the wonderful times we had with mom and be grateful we had her as long as we did. I am thankful for the life she has given me. I feel so blessed and grateful she was my mother. She was perfect in so many ways, and she made life perfect for us, just for having been in it. I thank God for her; for her warmth, her love, and her gentle presence.

I will finish with my Mom's final words because they express how I feel. "Thank you, Thank you, and Thank you."

Thank you, Mom.

◆ ◆ ◆

After leaving the funeral home, I went to Walmart and bought an exercise book. My favorite way to write seemed only fitting for Nurse Byrne. I had to handwrite my thoughts as my heart needed to feel the comfort only pen to paper can give to a writer.

At the Wake, there wasn't a rosary, but there were two priests, Father White and Father O'Quinn. I took comfort in seeing Father O'Quinn, as he had been my favorite priest growing up, and he had buried both my parents. Father White addressed the congregation and said a prayer, and then he invited anyone who had something to say about Nurse Byrne to come forward and share their thoughts about her. Several people shared their memories, and then I delivered my farewell to Nurse Byrne. To close this book, I would like to share it with you.

Farewell Nurse Byrne

What can I say about you that someone has not said before? Nothing. Last year, I thought of you when I taught a self-image workshop to women. I asked them to think of five women they admire and choose five qualities they have in common. The participants were to use these qualities to help them create a new self-image. I decided on one woman as she had all of the characteristics I admire in a person. The woman I chose was you, Nurse Sheila Byrne, and the five traits I decided to work on were only some of the many admirable qualities you have, but I would like to share them with everyone to remind them of your greatness.

You Were Kind, The Kindest Person I Have Ever Known.

You brought food to school to feed children who might be hungry. You brought banana bread and juice to the prenatal classes because the pregnant women deserved a treat. You spoke kindly to everyone, making him or her feel as if he or she was the most important person in the world while in your presence. You were a constant reminder that people might not remember what you did, but they will remember how you made them feel, as you made everyone feel special.

You Were Strong.

You raised five children on your own after your husband passed. You worked. You played. You loved; not only your children but all children. You knew when to be stern and when to have fun, 'just because.' I know you are smiling proudly tonight as your children are here together to celebrate your life, and as you told me, "families need each other, whether they realize it or not."

You Were Wise.

You seemed to have an answer for everything. You were well-read and interested in so many things. You never judged us, so we knew at school if we had a question we could ask you. You provided a 'safe space' long before anyone documented its importance, and your responses always came from a loving place.

You Were Graceful.

You were beautiful inside as well as outside and carried yourself with so much class. You dressed beautifully, spoke like a lady, and always kept yourself in check unless you thought someone was "being wronged," then you would speak out, or as you put it – you would overstep. I will never forget the story you shared with me about a situation that happened when you were a child. I hope you do not mind, but I am going to share that story. You told me that one day, a boy, known for stealing in the community, was in the process of taking money from a young girl when you caught him. You grabbed the money from him, and said, "Excuse me, that's my money," and walked away. Later you went back, found the girl, and returned the money to her. You said to me, "Never stand by and let people do bad things to others. You have to take action." The way you told me that story made me smile, as you were quite passionate about standing up for vulnerable people. When you finished the story, you recomposed yourself and said, "I may have overstepped a bit." You made me laugh because you were a master at keeping yourself in check, but your desire to help someone by righting a wrong was even stronger. You were so graceful. I never heard you say an unkind word about anyone. You found good in everyone and everything. You were a positive role model, and as described to me by your dearest friends, a real lady.

You Were Loving And Caring.

Everyone would describe you as a loving and caring person. You cared so much about others that you constantly put others' concerns at the forefront. You cared how we felt, what we needed, and how you could help. You were a natural caregiver, a loving person, and a gift to the world.

For everyone present tonight, remember, what we see in others is also present in ourselves; otherwise, we would not be able to recognize those qualities in another person. There is a little bit of Sheila Byrne in all of us; all we have to do is try a little harder to be more like her, and those characteristics will develop and grow within us. Nurse Byrne will never cease to be as we will carry on her consciousness because we are blessed to have shared a part of her life.

Death is not the end of life but the beginning of something new. If we take this perspective, we are aware that those who go before us stay here, as we carry them within us. We are all energy, and energy never dies, it just changes form.

While we are here celebrating the life of a Mother, Grandmother, Aunt, Friend, and Nurse, let us be grateful for her life and for the blessings we have received because she lived, and we were fortunate enough to have experienced it.

Although we have heavy hearts tonight, Nurse Byrne would want us to leave with an open heart because when you open your heart to everyone, no one is ever missing! I am eternally grateful for the opportunity to have known such an extraordinary person.

With Love and Gratitude,

Sheila

P.S. I hope these memories inspire others as you have inspired me.

Life Lessons From The Field

Soul Reflections: Let Go and Let God. When life gives you unwanted gifts, live from a place of love, and trust that there is a Divine Plan, and that it is always for the highest good. Do not be afraid to surrender to life's challenges. When you cast your burdens to the Lord, great things happen. Look back at life as a collection of memories shared with those you love. Always remember that we do not choose the conditions, but we do create the memories. How do you want to remember experiences with your loved one? Make great memories. Be kind to others, strong when you need to be, apply wisdom to your words, and always keep yourself in check. When you live each day as if it is your last, you will have no regrets. We can express gratitude daily by looking for blessings in everything, and that includes grief. There is a time to mourn, a time to live, and a time to be glad you did.

Soul Whispers

➢ Are you kind, and caring?

➢ Can you be strong when you need to be?

➢ Can you let go and surrender to a higher power

➢ Do you ever fall from grace?

➢ What would you do today if you knew it would be your last?

"And straightway coming up out of the water, he saw the heavens opened, and the Spirit like a dove descending upon him: And there came a voice from heaven, saying, Thou art my beloved Son (daughter), in whom I am well pleased."

Mark 1: 10-11(KJV)

AUGUST 5, 2019

The Day Nurse Sheila Maureen Byrne Went To Heaven.

Afterword

Nurse Byrne's niece Janet shared the following story with me after the funeral.

"When my mom passed, we went to my aunt Sheila's for lunch, and I noticed on the calendar hanging on the wall that she had written on the day my mom passed, The day Audrey Rose went to heaven."

Janet Byrne Turpin, as you were telling me this story, I imagined the last page of this book, and when I returned home, the first thing I did was write on my calendar under August 5, 2019, "the day Nurse Byrne went to heaven." The second thing I did was write the last page of this book.

Thank you for sharing that memory with me.

ABOUT THE AUTHOR

Sheila Trask is a lifelong learner and educator who spends her time reading, writing, and discovering new ways to help others realize their full potential. She teaches at the College of the North Atlantic, is a Gratitude Life Coach, a Motivational Speaker, and a Community Activist. Because of her transformation, Sheila shares her passion for personal growth and development through writing, teaching, and speaking. Born and raised in Stephenville, she still loves the sound of the ocean and hearing the voice of her son Jacob Vaughn Trask saying, "Mom."

Sheila is the author of The Gratitude Attitude, the first book in her series Life Lessons from the Field.

To learn more about Sheila go to www.sheilatrask.com

Life Lessons From The Field

My goal is to create at least six books for this series, which teaches people how to live a better life by learning from life experiences. These lessons may open your eyes, heal your soul, or empower you to lead your life as an inspirational person.

Works Cited

Allen, J. (1903). As a Man Thinketh. Camarillo: DeVorss Publications.

Archival Moments. (2020, 08 04). Retrieved from Little Dale: http://archivalmoments.ca/tag/littledale/

Chopra, D. (2009). Reinventing the Body, Resurrecting the Soul. New York: Harmony Books.

Choquette, S. (2005). Trust Your Vibes: Secret Tools for Six-Sensory Living.

Carlsbad: Hay House.

Courtney, B. (2020, 08, 04). Barns-Courtney-fire-lyrics. Retrieved from Genius: https://genius.com/Barns-courtney-fire-lyrics

Emerson, R. W. (2020). Compensation by Ralph Waldo Emerson. Retrieved from Emersoncentral: https://emersoncentral.com/texts/essays-first-series/compensation/

Farmer, S. D. (2006). Animal Spirit Guides. Carlsbad: Hay House.

First World War Gallery Portraits Index. (2020, 08 04). Retrieved from Heritage NF: https://www.heritage.nf.ca/firstworldwar/gallery/portraits/index

Hay, L. (1984). You Can Heal Your Life. Carlsbad: Hay House.

Maltz, M. (2001). The New Psycho-Cybernetics. New York: Prentice Hall Press. Ponder, C. (2011). The Dynamic Laws of Prosperity. CT: Martino Publishing.

Quintilianus, M. F. (2020, July 20). Quotes. Retrieved from Quotes: https://www.quotes.net/quote/43788

The Holy Bible - King James Version. (n.d.). United States: Collins World.

Veteran-Suicide Mortality Study, 2018. (2020, 08 04). Retrieved from Veterans.gc.ca: https://www.veterans.gc.ca/eng/about-vac/research/research-directorate/publications/reports/veteran-suicide-mortality-study2018

Made in the USA
Middletown, DE
19 March 2021